JMWW

Masthead

Editor-in-Chief and Founding Editor: Jen Michalski
Senior Poetry Editor: CarlaJean Valluzzi
Senior Fiction Editor: Michael Tager
Senior Creative Nonfiction Editor: Cassandra Osvatics
Contributing Poetry Editor: Ashlie Kauffman Sarsgard
Contributing Nonfiction Editor: Hannah Grieco
Associate Poetry Editors: Fitz Fitzgerald, Jessica Lynn Dotson
Associate Fiction Editors: Margaret Adams, Robin Bissett, Rachel Farber, Charlie Hope-D'Anieri, Madison Krchnavy, Julieanne Larick, Maryam Shadmehr, Maxwell Suzuki, Addie Tsai
Associate Flash Fiction Editors: Kristin Bonilla, Laura Huey Chamberlain, Jolene McIlwain, Silas Jones
Associate Creative Nonfiction Editors: Shareen Murayama, Juliet Way-Henthorne
Past Editors: Catherine Harrison (co-founding editor), Megan Calhoun, Alyce Lomax, Oana Capota, David Hills, Erin Vachon, Linda Wastila, Alle Hall, Andrea Appleton, Andrew McDowell, Anna Moore, Becca Borawski Jenkins, Briana Wingate, Dario DiBattista, Gavin Colton, Girija Sankar, Ingrid Jendrzejewski, Lesley Heiser, Lituo Huang, Michael Blackburn, Pj Dominiski, Sierra Troy-Regier, W.F. Lantry, Allie Bowerman, Andie Schoenfeld, Anya Schwartz, aureleo sans, Bailey Drumm, Caroliena Cabada, Dakotah Jennifer, Madeline St. Clair, Danielle Brundage, Kimi Hardesty, Nathan Pensky, Sandy Wilbur, Shelby Newsome, Steven Genise, Talia Military, Sebastian Bronson Boddie, Kara Moskowitz, Jenny Sadre-Orafai, Jenny Sadre-Orafai

JMWW

A MODERN TIMES ANTHOLOGY

JEN MICHALSKI, EDITOR

MODERN
TIMES

TABLE OF CONTENTS

2014

2015

2016

2022

EDITORIAL PREFACE

When I started *jmww* in 2002, I wasn't really thinking. I mean, I wasn't thinking that we'd be around for twenty years. Mostly, I started *jmww* to connect with people. I'd just graduated with a Master's Degree in Professional Writing, and I missed the fiction workshops I'd attended with my fellow graduates. I missed reading short stories and talking about them. I missed the camaraderie and encouragement we received and gave each other. I asked two other graduates of my program—Catherine Harrison, and, later, Megan Calhoun—whether they'd be interested in starting an online journal. I bought one of those *HTML for Dummies* books and put together a rudimentary website over a weekend. I created an Excel spreadsheet for our submissions. And we were off! Our first issue contained three stories—one from Catherine, one from Alyce Lomax, who later became a fiction editor at *jmww*, and one was a creative nonfiction piece I'd solicited from a friend. I created some, well, interesting, illustrations on Paint to accompany the stories.

Since then, we've grown from a quarterly to a weekly journal. Our stories have appeared as honorable mentions in *Best American Essays*, and have also been selected for *Best Small Fictions*, the Wigleaf Top 50, BIFFY, Best of Net, and the VERA. We've released six print anthologies and three hand-assembled poetry chapbook contest winners. We've offered online workshops and attended local, regional, and national writers' conferences, talking to you from behind the vendors' tables, over a lectern during a talk, or next to you at the bar. We're thinking of starting a writers' conference on the West Coast. We're even hoping to pay contributors as early as next year—while keeping submissions free.

EDITORIAL PREFACE

We're so grateful to have gotten to know you and published your work over the last twenty years, and we're also grateful to be publishing yet another print anthology, this time in conjunction with Modern Times Publishing. It picks up in 2013, where our last anthology left off, and includes the best work we've published over the last decade, as voted on by our editors. It's been such a pleasure to work with everyone at Modern Times, and going through almost a decade of work has reminded me how much I love what we do here, enough that, this time around, I *am* thinking—I'm thinking I could see us doing this for another twenty years. Talk to you in 2042—

Jen Michalski
Editor in Chief

2013

THE BONE HOUSE

C. SAMUEL REES

This cross hasn't held the weight
so well all these years.

From within, its boney, iron core
has shed the molded concrete

like days from recent memory,
the name, always blurry, now no more

than a gentle ridge. Spooling wire
wraps tight what little remains

of the iron and stone body. Other graves
are niches, houses' empty doors,

where spirits crouch from rain,
sun, the spitting cold. Others

are raised coffins sprouting from the earth
like topographic scars left unmarked

on the map. And out in Nebraska
four cedars grow instead of fence

2013

posts to hedge in ghosts, hungry
or not. And the bone houses full with

jars and suitcases and shoeboxes
well-fed on dust and rags.

They wait for their journey home.
They wait to be justly risen,

taken by a descendant they never
met to a village they long

forgot, like fog forgets
the trees when it lifts its veil.

There are no bones left for my grandfather.

There is no exhuming; no zinc housed
coffin, embalmed skin—

no chance of meeting. He's sown
in his garden, his ashy seeds long washed

away. A seed's a casket, it opens
only in the earth

even as it is washed off into
a ditch where chrysanthemums grow,

their buds clusters like bones
in an ossuary.

My brother told me epitaphs
were speaking stones—dumb but

always talking. What stones tell
is all for others, audience-bound.

Headstones like parcels in the bone house,
waiting to be read and carried

away in mind and memory.

Who can see this lattice work
of blood? Or hear the clutters and sounds

of us laughing quietly, tears
like birthmarks, around the casket.

My cousin asking:
"Are you really sad that he's dead?"

her eyes wild like the white of
Queen Anne's Lace. My grandmother,

a wisp,

spitting over and over "I'm just so mad at him.
Just so mad. Just so mad."

We all come up short.

When I was a boy I would do violence
to hills of shale stone,

scrambling up its fish scaled back.
I would choke down blooms

of dust and slivered rocks.
Some stones would slip and break

below as I raced for the top, scattering
a dozen arrowhead pieces in the dirt.

My hands bled with buried splinters.
He's not buried in a farmer's

field, nestled up close with lost
flint arrows, lost hoe tips,

petrified moles.
Families of bull frogs

freeze themselves in a burning
cold lake when winter rises.

Below their sleeping is absence.

Their black-brown eyes are lamps
lit only for the first thaw, buried

until it all turns to slurry and forgets
them as we wriggle and fight

to the surface mud where they
are buried under the sky, reeds,

and warming air. Dancing
in the muck, eyes bulging,

croaking, rigid from long cold.
Unfolding, again living.

Why should anyone tell me
what is, what is, what is,

voice breaking like the curse
of firecrackers bursting on long strings

to ward off the dead.

It is raining. The mud pools in the yard.
I stand high on the porch and he

crouches in his niche beneath his holly
tree. He is a shadow because he is draped

in a white shower curtain his .22
jutting like a bone, like a portent,

ghost, forgotten
antler white and cast-off

in the field. My eyes grow dim
as I watch: he raises the rifle

and the world cracks. He is so far
away and in the rain. The small unseen

creature howls then cuts its howl.
My eyes grow dim

and it's only the kiss of the holly tree
and the man draped in white I see.

In low places the air grows
thin, not up high like it's said,

a hand slips through the cracks,
a votive offer, a chance deformity.

2013

Take his hand

and draw the fragment through.
It's not so heavy now.

This end-song lacks the weight
it once bore. Take that hand

and wrap it softly in a rag, leave
its bad shadow on the concrete,

let it clatter away like tin cans
cut loose from their strings.

Take up dirt in handfuls
and lay down that piece of him

beneath the holly tree,
in his niche. Let one, two,

three knife-tipped leaves scatter
over him
                    as covering dirt.

VARET STREET, OCTOBER

MONICA WENDEL

I can't say I minded
the mosquito last night—
he seemed intimately
knowledgeable of us,
and it was his wings
that woke us at an hour,
indeterminate, from
where we could find
each other, hands
to ears or twisting hair
and was it then that
we spoke? Without
sex, I dreamed of sex
in the bed we were
in, realized that it was
the first time we had
fallen asleep together
to the sound of rain—

across the way, a light
was on, rare, lace
curtains, and in
the morning I saw
a woman on the ground

2013

floor sewing at a
machine, the projects
rising like great forest
trees a quarter mile
away, we are dependent,
the video had said,
dependent on the government
to provide for us
what we do not
provide for ourselves
and though we
had watched the video
together I thought
of my father falling
yesterday, his ankle
or his hip buckling,
I thought of my sister
bandaging burned
hands from trash-can
fires, and pant legs,
one part of the body
frozen, the other aflame,
even in the home
we make next to
the paintings and
the graffiti we must
suffer so much loss.

LABYRINTH 17

OLIVER DE LA PAZ

The boy in the labyrinth smells the musk of the beast. It hangs in the arches of corridors, heavy like a spiced foam. The pang of it singes the boy's eyes. He thinks of peppercorns crunched between his back molars, the way the flavor lingers on his tongue, spiking up into his nasal cavity. The smell bursts into his eyes and they tear. Around him the things of the lair. A child's skull. A shoe. A matte of hair. Somewhere the beast lowers his head and sharpens the points of his horns against the labyrinth stone. Somewhere the beast cleaves the air with his scent. Here, his smell swirls about the bone-strewn alcove. The boy in the labyrinth lifts the bottom of his shirt up to cover his nose and mouth. And in the lair, the vortex of a presence spins its pungent cyclone.

LABYRINTH 5

OLIVER DE LA PAZ

The boy in the labyrinth is lost. And it is not by chance. He is here to find the beast, maker of accident and conservator of bones. At night, the boy listens to his body. The gardens of blood along his carotid. The march of his pulse into the blue garlands of his wrists. What a terrible place to lie awake and listen, he thinks. Terrible, to be lost within the spirals of the ear. Somewhere, the beast keeps time with its paces, antechamber to antechamber. The sound of his horns rub against marble. In a darkness such as this, old countries and new countries die and are born. And the labyrinth's causeways kiss their darkness, long and hard. Its own eyes shut tight.

LABYRINTH 28

OLIVER DE LA PAZ

The boy in the labyrinth sees shadows on the wall. They move with his torch, forming different animals. The bird. The rabbit. The dog. So many aspects of the surface world. This makes him sad. He feels the pain of seeing something beautiful. Which is a sort of physical form. The pain is a layer. Having spent a great deal of time in the dark, the shadows are multiples of beauty. Because there is a thickness to this beauty, the boy feels the weight on his heart. Which is like an internal longing or the presence of a word on the tip of his tongue. A word under a heavy geology, like the striations of rock. The stripes of rock shift under the shadows. The bird is flying. The rabbit is hopping. The dog is running. All of these shadows make the boy in the labyrinth heart-sick. Make him hum.

CAUSE AND EFFECT

MONTY JONES

How, after all, can one thing cause another?
I know I can strike a match and burn a prairie
and every rough barn and chicken coop with it,
driving every owl and lark out of its home,

but how do I get hold of the match to begin with,
or come into the desire to see the world in flames,
or wake up one day after another only to find
everything still in place, longing for destruction?

How can I be the one standing between a past
and future, the fulcrum on which all turns, the first
leaning domino in a setup that runs across a room,
through a charred landscape, over the red horizon?

How does it happen that the world will wake up
and decide to try again, rather than go back to sleep?

OH, HOW I LOVED YOU ...

SHERINE GILMOUR

I loved the way you made me weak, asleep
by 8 pm. Then the way you'd wake me, dry heaving.
The gas you gave me, bad as toxic fumes
that sent Nick to the other room,
laughing. At the grocery, I picked the apple
with the reddest cheeks. Someday I would pack you lunches.
I wanted to paint your room with songbirds, gulls,
string paper airplanes from the ceiling in bunches.
You made me determined. Oh, love! Heavy bells of my breasts.
Every object I touched became a touch closer to you,
so that our home became layers of touches.
The first time the midwife said,
"Come in so we can check, right away,"
                    your heart clapped loudly, defiantly *Yes-yes-yes!*

BIRD BOX

MK SUKACH

for Christina

Broken wing.
It is always six o'clock or seven, Sunday
or Monday, October, this year or another
in a bird box with penciled-out holes
through which just enough light passes
like the uncertainty that every hour could be
a decade spilling from the cup of your hands.

Interruption.
Nothing seems to change between two men talking
without saying anything but understanding everything
until the waitress interrupts what they are not saying
and at least one looks up to say what he'll have.

Geometry.
Everything spins in the street. The Black Lab, for example,
turning tighter circles directly proportional to the radius
of the leash a woman is desperately trying to correct
by reversing her spin on the ball of her opposing foot.

Reflection.
Can't think about much else when you find a bird

in your living room, which is still unpainted, lamps
and chairs a party huddled together in the center;
and there's the book you lost, or thought you lost.

The Bird.
A bird cradled to your chest will listen to your heart.
The emergency animal clinic nurse understands this.
Try to imagine a quiet way of saying you were amazing.
Think he will be alright? And I want it to be true. *Yes.*

Words.
After a late dinner, a silence during the drive home,
I wanted to say something silly about the two men seated
next to us in the restaurant or the woman pirouetting
with her dog in the street. The breath comes without
words. The bed is where we talk. So, I wait till then.

Hands.
You hand me my toothbrush, I pass you the toothpaste.
We are married like that. I'm still awake when your bird
hand settles on my chest. *I can feel your heart beating.*
Little bird heart, I think. Some hands are expert at this.

AN EDUCATION IN LETTERS

JANE LIN

Last night I told Rosemary
what she'd wanted to know—mimed the bear
tasting honey from a hive.
She'd said to ask Sevanna

who had described only A to me, her arms
snapping shut like an alligator snout.
But B, rubbery, buttery, bendable B
bounced against Rosemary's dying body.

Reversal from strawberry ice cream,
from walking the two steps
from potty seat to bed, making me promise
to let her pay for the round wood

toothpicks and Chapstick so good
for hospital lips. My hand clumsy on hers.
My words too, like epistles to the dead. And so
the grieving begins for the 97-year-old

kindergarten teacher, widowed
and childless. In the morning,

a sterile room. Standing
I wait for a nurse to acknowledge me,

tell me what I already see
because I can't leave like a nobody
                                   no one notified. No letter. Nothing.

QUESTIONS AND ANSWERS

JANE LIN

The public relations officer from the charity chanted
in a language I didn't understand. There were gestures
and clapping. I stood at the head of the hospital bed,
brushed a hand over my mother's hair because a woman
had done this to me in my grief a month before at an A&W
on a hillside in Vermont
                              and I had found it comforting.

My mother twitched her head in irritation, too weak
to move her arms, to speak. I knew then I was nobody.
Only the friend in her blue uniform could rouse a response
near the end, some rallied squeeze of the hand.

We waited once, at home, the others preparing the car, the bags,
for the ER. She asked me if I had any questions. I said no.

Still no, the possible answers irrelevant.
                                        Did you love him?
Bitter melon—
                  the waxed nubbly skin, orange-tinged flesh,
                        rough seeds in their slipcases
—shocked when she considered he might miss her
                                                    slipped free
                              of our binds.

ECOSTATION FOR DISPOSAL AND RECYCLING

JANE LIN

The shrink wrap on the Happy Lantern
split open, nine years on a bedroom door knob.
The Whistling Flower sat intact, a squat
triangular box. The man in the booth
said he'd hold them for Hazardous Waste
though the sign read No Fireworks.

I was feeling the alternate universe—
the fountaining sparks, the screaming
as something streamed, burned away.
American alternative to red chains
of firecrackers, rapid rat-a-tat to scatter
spirits from a wedding.

I handed them over, disposed of at last,
their use wrong in the weeks after 9/11, wrong
in the drought years that followed. The gown
right, groom, guests—only three fearful of flying.
And the spirits? An ordinary allotment
of luck and misfortune in our marriage

2013

but for my mother, the intersection
of our married lives measured in visits, calls.
Even in childhood there are unknown hours
passed between Mother and Father. He says,
"When our first was born, her sisters
could not come to help, and I did not ask

my family. I thought, She is strong."
He dwells in that place outside our knowledge,
speaks her name in a voice I never knew,
to the urn's fragment spirit that remembers
while the rest cycles to the next life
improved, having suffered, burned away.

WEIGHT OF ABUNDANCE

IRIS JAMAHL DUNKLE

On days when sun blazes hills awake,
when still damp earth aches dark possibilities,
when crooked teeth of dilapidated barns
and crumbling stucco of lost missions
hum with stories they cannot forget,
I look at my freckled hands and try to find
a cartography for this desire to know
that seems stitched into me, into any
who live where one wakes to a horizon
that is continually blurred by low fog.
Stories are as abundant as the trees
and vines that are repeatedly heavy
with fruit. *What to dig up? What is enough?*
In a garden so thick with weeds, sustenance
bleeds with what is pressing upon it. So
days slur past, fat and happy, until
the eye sights it driving past, or the hoe
upturns the hidden artifact, revealing
another history buried underneath.

OWLING

JAMES GRINWIS

Owls come in many shapes.
Strigiformes, they are called.
One is cold then hot then a latch
of warmth, very much
like a short-eared owl. A burrowing
owl. A snowy one. The tiara discing
through the window in resplendent
diatomaceous sunlight shone
like Carlos's hand kilned white
by the highway noon.
Encirclings are aspects of hawks,
very un-owl, whose strikes are more silent,
sudden, and barbed. I knifed into the
urban woodland and found a frozen
waterfall and imagined an ancient god
heaving against the rounded hills
which were like frozen hulls.
An incidental music filtered
through my left cerebrum and soothed
the paleolithic stem, so I went home.
The dog and his hundred pounds swelled
with happiness. My neighbor had wandered in
and left a note about wanting
some wine, and in return for the box of Cabernet

she'd given my big hearted hound
a bath with the watering can and a bar of soap.
His eyes were like globes
holding inside them the blood of a saint.
I used to believe the souls of athletes
matched the utensils of their sport.
Baseball: hard with a barely discernible shell;
golf: swift and devastating; basketball:
sweat-smashed and pocked; puck: a tough,
spit-strewn stone; endurance athletes with nothing
except slices of water, land, and air.
But we were speaking of owls, their airy,
fluffed up forms, their deadliness and instinct for love.

STOPPING BY THE DRUGSTORE FOR A BAG OF PINK RAZORS

AMORAK HUEY

Oh the things we do for luck. I've been late shifting at the bar,
another uneventful episode pouring hardluck drinks

for those seeking forgiveness, or permission:
beerspill, sweatstain, stale tobacco, uneasy glances

at my elbow tattoos. Breathe in this polluted sweep—
what passes for fresh air. My city, my time of night,

my shortcuts & streetlights. We've all done these scenes:
cat knocks over trash can & our hero relaxes

thinking danger past. We've all fallen in love
with the same three stars: those bright enough

to shove through the haze. One day I woke
& it had been a long time since I'd told

my favorite jokes, you know, women
& batteries, foxes & elephants—not even

faintly amusing anymore & anyone who thinks
people don't change hasn't seen my bald spot.

I am a long way from sleep: neon storefront, all-hours pharmacy,
at home a woman who cares enough to shave her legs,

& something resembling ordinary
burbling through the cracks in the sidewalks.

In the distance a siren. Another possibility unfolding.

NORTHERN LIGHTS

BRAD EFFORD

Pock-marked home of tractors
on the highways, emerald and gold,

northern Minnesota preens
in the summer, celebrates its nights'

dramatic chills, the baying of coyotes.
We buy swimsuits extra long, DEET

ourselves just inside the dilapidating screen
door, and step out to gather stones

for polishing in the shallow riverbed—
they glitter dull as unburied gems when

we hold them to the sun. In July,
Moose Lake is still polar-cold, better suited

for arctic terns than long-limbed, sun-
burned boys. We sprint across its pebble

shore to warm up on the way, blood rushing
smart through our bodies, fast enough

to get us to the water. Here we've spent
half our lives scraping dried blood

from old bug bites, crossing the high grass
to the outhouse after midnight, the moon

bear-sized, *aurora borealis*, though
faint, across the sky—we see ourselves

too much in every fearsome thing.
Bands of colors we thought we knew

before, we know no other way now: fire-pink
and -blue, pale green of dragonfly

wings, orange of the bottoms of our feet.
Fourth-grade skipper. Animal bone

collector. We watched each other grow,
and grew. Sent letters home on old newsprint

and bathed with the door half-cracked
for the steam, posing in the mirror palmed

clean, three hairs apiece sprouting
thin as ripped-out beetle legs

from the concave of our chests. We raced
everywhere—to the barn loft, the dinner

bell, the thin-skinned feral dogs sniffing
clover on the roadside. We bolted

from the kneeling stance, made for
the lake unbound by light, and dove.

NAILS

JEREMY PENNA

Uncle Ivan got cancer, and he said his skin
got so soft the rain hitting it would leave a bruise.
I think that of today where only the angled breeze
crimping the puddle makes the dark rain
visible as it sprawls on the lawn, sops below.
Once, he lugged in the Atlantic cold,
the weather taxing holes in his gumshoes,
the iron boxes of nails to load on the hi-lo.
Come nails in the weather. Come nails down.
His laughter full of nails as he laughed alone
on the bed, skin mottled with jaundice,
hurting on the shore of himself, a snared fish.
Each thought hits and hits, now, without fail
the painful and exact nerve of the funny bone.

LEAVES

JEREMY PENNA

Dear Jesus, I'm sick of my boss and I miss
my mother. No, Earth can't revolve around me,
but what's the sun, what's gravity, what's entropy
have that I don't? They make the green grass.
They don't know they're doing it. Ask my boss
who she'd rather have work for her, entropy or me.
I'd be lying if I said that it wouldn't be dead close.
But I'd win. Look, give my mother back to me
for one day and you can take me a year sooner.
The sun, gravity, entropy, they don't negotiate.
Surely you must. You did. I'll tell you what,
I'll slave away forever if once in a blue moon,
you'd make a leaf in the wind elevate,
stick to the wound of the twig and turn green.

TRUCK PICTURE, 1962

ROY BENTLEY

Some love is like an aperture—
hearts open and close, allow the lens
of self and memory-film to take the light
at different intensities. It's still love.

My father is smiling. There's a sign on the side
of a '57 Ford Ranchero truck reading *Roy's Shell*.
An address and phone number in red-lettered script.
He's at the wheel, window down. My sister Suzanne
calls attention to a shadow, a vertical-running line.
As from tape. As if the negative was ripped. Torn.

And I remember blood flowing from his face after
she struck him; that time, for bringing a woman
along. They were divorcing but would remarry.
That night, he was stopping by to drop me off.
That weekend, my sisters hadn't gone with him.
I recall that he opened my door. Said, "Hurry!"

I'm sure the woman was sitting next to him.
I'm sure she was difficult to get to because
my mother tried to reach across me to hit her
and hit me. I come from those who strike first,

which is to say, my mother did. Her mother,
my granny, absorbed a blow. Cried and cried.

The violence of desire is understandable but tough
to do much about, if you're a kid. I see my father
tearing out of the driveway, sparks arcing up
from underneath the Ranchero, rooster-tailing
into an Ohio night I enter again and again,
trying to frame and snap a picture I trust.

LAST THINGS

ROY BENTLEY

At dusk in the nursing home the light outside
turned golden, burnished. Car windshields
beaded rain and a hooded jogger on Main Street
flashed a glance my way, from street to window.

Her arms opened like a pair of emaciated wings
to say that she loved me now and would forever.
She said it aloud. I thought *What's this about?*—
and that gold light fell like a blessing or glowed.

In a month they would hook her up to oxygen,
not a body but an emptiness into which they could
pour their Medicare-expensive morphine and water
from a scarlet sponge, my mother become a sepulcher

complete with wind sound reminiscent of hollowness
and any blustery late afternoon in that part of Ohio.
I'd have to call that vacancy Mother. Hold its hand.
I could've taken her picture by the window that day

instead of the one I had snapped in my Harley jacket
when a roomful of March air was a house of breath.
Now, only in imaginings do I hear her say that there
is an abundance of adoration allocated to each body

but that we must know to claim it with an embrace
as a glimpsed world rushes by over our shoulders,
our time together recognizable as fleeting forms:
the look from a stranger running past in the rain.

TROUBADOUR

EVE STRILLACCI

Tell me again how the front door fluttered
like a wing, you, the boy, drawn through
the dark depths of the house as a pendulum
flies through its coffin of hours. Tell me again
how time buries us, memory's blind horse tilling

the backyard for bones. Give me the bodies,
Father, offer simulacrum: our stories.
Your mother kept a garden. You were seeded,
green and lovely, like a knight. She tended
turrets of tomatoes, spires of string beans,

translucent cabbage, buds like rooted pearls.
Pheasants barked from the butcher's block,
Grandfather's pets, a richly blooded meal
for poor Poles like yourselves, but you ate well,
better, even, than your brothers, hungry always

for the summer and her slick stone fruits—
a plum, a pear, whose tender flesh protects
a lignifying heart. Turn it back, turn it over,
show the roots that grew the forest, promise me
secrets, promise godliness, a nurse. Were we

a family of romantics? Were we brave? Once
you fenced through a hustle of bees to save
a neighbor. Twice you were married. Three times
you were thrown from memory's old horse.
Keep digging, Father. The corpse! The corpse!

PRODIGAL

EVE STRILLACCI

Mother ladles soup into a china bowl—a fall
minestrone: sweet moons of carrot, cradled onions

rocking softly in the salted broth. Diced peppers
the color of sea kelp swim to the surface, exotic fishes

kissing the cornflower hem, innocent of their
vulnerability. A hawk might seize them, curl his toes

in the shallow bed and feast, but the tree in the back
yard is gone now, taken in the storm, so there's no place

for him to eat, no jointed branch on which to settle.
Ice clobbered the dogwood. For days the tree bowed

to the gale, bridged the frigid air to scar snow with her
branches—kneeled like a peasant before some king. Mother

is tired tonight. She sets the first aside, floods mine
with rosemary and root vegetables before serving herself

a generous scoop—salt and steam for the living. Outside,
the bare stump stands accusing, while a hungry hawk coasts

through clouds burdened with snow. *Why is it you, and not the tree returning?* Because everybody needs somewhere to go.

SOUTHERN HEAT

KELLY MCQUAIN

It was my step-grandfather who said the word
as we drove through a blur of Georgia peanut fields
past black kids sitting on shanty stoops:
a boy and girl not much older than me—
cornrow hair, dirt on their feet. And though
I'd never heard the word before that family visit south,
I knew what it meant the moment
my grandfather opened his mouth. Hot wind
through the window wouldn't blow it away.
My fault? I was the one who'd made him say
"Them's jigaboos" when I pointed
out the window to ask *Who're they?*

I couldn't offer the awkward chuckle
someone else in the car did—my mother?
older brother? I knew their hiccup of laughter hid
the same disappointment I felt in this man.
He didn't understand: *words hurt.* I did.
At seven, I already knew "faggot", I knew "queer".
I knew my step-grandfather, studying to be a preacher,
had his own messed-up cross to bear
having lost his first wife and six kids nine years before
in a house fire while he was out working
the railroad graveyard shift.

Difference burned, too —I knew the sting of its blisters—
yet hot Georgia dust clawed at my throat
as my granddad's car tore down that gravel road.
Houses and fields swept by. Light whipped
like a cotton sheet. I sat down, the hot vinyl seat
burning me. I was burning alive!
Damn if I didn't hate everyone
the way I hated myself inside.

Our gas was low so we stopped
at an old clapboard store to pee and fill up.
While Grandpop stood working the pump
my brother and I followed the women
past a beat-up cigar store Indian
into the store's dusty cool
where amber fly strips stirred like streamers
above the sweep of an oscillating fan.
What I didn't understand
was how
putting down a person could prop another up.
No one to ask, so instead
I begged Mama for a grape pop.
She hunted for coins as Grandpop strode in
to shoot the shit with the storekeeper.
All hellfire, all brimstone, my grandpop.
In a few years, he'd make one lousy preacher.
He paid for the gas, my grape Nehi.
My love? That went unearned.
I pressed the cold bottle to my chest as I left
but damn if we still didn't burn.

2014

SELECTED FROM ICE / LAND

DEVON WOOTTEN

What's said of stones, that they, indurate,
confirm what we have long suspected—

the sequel, the consequence—repetition
to an almost indefinite extent.

As in *days & yet more days,*
days upon days, and days without number…

O stones, O unstinting ampersands,
ageless, smooth, & heavy in the hand—

what of *now*? What of *here & this &*
Is my love for her geological?

Whence this compensatory alikeness,
when our bodies, these unbearable

remainders, insist upon this moment, numinous & undivided.

A BIRD COMES CLOSE

DAVID MOHAN

A bird came close on our lawn.
I don't stir. I am sunbathing,
dazzled by the lines of fences.
This bird stops, lost and wild
in the grasses' resistance.
I almost expect a peck on my skin,
the scrabble of wings upsetting
dark glasses, but I am in my dream—
a bird has come out of the last elm
in a time with no gardens—
it carries seed like a message,
pours birdsong in the shell
of my ear, its sound like traffic
of the ocean.

THE TOMB OF LADY FU HAO

BARBARA DANIELS

It's the kind of day when all the stories
seem to include me, servants killed
to accompany Fu Hao into the afterlife,
Saint Francis blinded by weeping.

I watch my butterfly bush produce one
purple efflorescence, wait for a pipevine
butterfly as if something beautiful
will land in a moment on my hands.

What comes in the doors and
windows seems to be music,
finding notes, sustaining them.
Son, I never imagined you.

When I thought of a child, I told
a tale of a girl in a red dress, a lamb
struggling out of her arms. What
would a boy do? Fish in the gutter?

Search dirt for coins? At the end
of the day, laughing, crying,
I seem to be caught in the general
burning, holding a flaming lyre.

2014

Fu Hao sits down among her cosmetics,
bone hairpins, cowry shells, bronze owl,
her cat on the bed. What gives solace?
The wind in its long dark dress.

SELF-PORTRAIT AS A WOODEN BIRD

BARBARA DANIELS

I'm capable of flight and of waiting,
talons, scaled legs, the rest of me
not fully risen from dark wood.

If I called, it would be music
you could hear nowhere else,
high notes a trumpet crying,

softer sounds a rosewood recorder
brought to your lips. I have a brutal beak.
I was the bird in the hand, made, sold.

I can't remember why I wait here,
watching you turn in the night, rise,
dress. Sometimes a curtain opens.

A cardinal comes to the window.
The false cherry blooms. Wasps tap
the glass. Something cracks inside me.

I know what's possible with axes, chisels,
knives. Make me again, carnal, knowing.
Lady, save me. You are passionate,

2014

give all for love, look unblinking toward
your own death. I fly into funneled
darkness, a bit of driftwood carried by wind.

MY HAND ON THE PHONE

BARBARA DANIELS

I wanted to tell you about the bluebirds
by the ballfield, the way they look
at me, wary but also curious.

My eyes water more since the surgery.
I carry Kleenex as you did, find them
in the dryer, stuck to the pants and socks.

You'd be surprised by the warnings
now—hazmats, lightning, tornados.
Fuel spilled into Big Timber Creek.

A friend told me that when she was
cooking, she called her mother just
to make sure she got everything right.

One afternoon she took out peppers
and onions and had her hand
on the phone before she remembered.

There's a new little bridge in the park.
They call it a box culvert. Frogs
gather below it, urgently calling.

WHO NEEDS A SHADOW

ALEXANDRA DALEY

Who needs a shadow—
              I have you:
       arms folded around me like quilted wings,
           a meadow of chest laced
           into my backbone.

Flutterings brush
behind my breasts—a hummingbird awakened
to fill stalled space
with Vivaldi's Four Seasons. Can you hear the violins?
                              Notes brighten my pulse,
or is that your ashless breath kindling my neck
or your peach-skinned fingers inking
                    I love you
                 across my collarbone.

In the distance a horizon is reassembling:
splintered flocks solidify into an arrow, hunched grass blades roll up their spines,
all the breakages cohered by your hold,
                    darkness ebbed.

BEHIND A GROVE

DANA YOST

A hard, hard life,
the pioneers,
sod-busters,
turning earth
one row at a time,
pulling plow by hand,
or, if they somehow squeezed
the money, behind a raggedy horse.
Winters froze cattle to death
standing up,
turned babies' skin red, then blue,
then black:
bury them after the thaw.
If diphtheria sweeps through,
takes every child,
you burn their clothes,
douse the bodies
with lye,
bury them together.
White angel. Fire angel.
Where my grandmother was born,
every building is now gone—the wood rotted,
or borrowed for another place,
the grove haggard,

and behind it, a pioneer cemetery,
half-dozen plots unmarked,
two holding the bones of children
lumped together in 1893,
others with the limestone markers
fallen, cracked, blackened,
names almost smeared smooth, illegible,
by wind, rain, time.
An Eagle Scout has been restoring it,
hammering in new fencing,
cementing in a new flag pole,
sifting death certificates to at least
list the names on a poster.
My blood down in those holes,
or some of it—my grandmother's cousins,
aunts, uncles.
I've had my photo taken near the flagpole
and a metal-pipe cross painted white.
Always in the summer, though, the photos.
Behind me, in one shot, the marker
for a woman named Mary
is prone in the prairie grass,
split horizontally. She died
at nineteen
in a winter month.

LUMBER

WILLIAM FARGASON

There were no plans: you constructed
as you went.
   Two-by-four by two-by-four;
nail by nail.
   First, the foundation:—
leveling the concrete, flagging the beams

for the next floor; why bother?—
no need to caulk the tub
      or wait for

the sheetrock dust to settle before
painting:—each step done out of order.

You climbed the ladder
     two stories
with a fifty pound bag of tar-backed shingles
on your shoulders to drive each flap down

with plastic-capped ½" nails
on a roof you had yet to build.

Then, you stood back and sketched the plans
based on what you had built.

2014

You had no idea how to
craft stairs mid-air from one level down

to the next. A two-by-four, if placed and nailed
here, makes a step; if here, a gate.
                                      But your father
was in your ear the whole time, accusing

you of not tossing the scraps out the windows
right—(it was right arm lower than left, then

use the leverage
                  of gravity to heave upwards)—
but you didn't listen. He was wrong.

You hung wiring around the fiberglass insulation,
skin itching from its shards—;

your vision that was the lack of a vision:
the constant leaks from rain dripping in

through cracks between sheets
of particleboard,—

and your father, outside, yelling

at you over the noise of the miter saw,
a voice you could almost now not hear.

GETTING THERE

NICOLE CALLIHAN

It's not easy to get to the other side of the glass.
I can't break it. I'm not strong enough.
I can't even throw a ball, let alone a man, a party.
Only once have I witnessed someone throwing time.
It was right before the end. My mother, of course.
Another time, I heard someone throw his voice.
He had a brain tumor and would die before summer.
He made the fish in the aquarium speak to me.
Nicole? The fish said. Psst… Nicole? Hey Nicole!!!
We were in a room full of people drinking coffee.
I was fifteen and worried that I had lost my mind
so I said nothing. I didn't say, *Anyone else hear the fish talking?*
Instead I snuck into the kitchen and stuck my thumb
into a strange pie. To get to the other side of the glass,
I would have to get out of my chair, walk down a long hallway,
pass the lab, go through the glass double doors,
swing a right, another right. Then maybe
I could stand on the back of whatever animal
sleeps soundlessly beneath my window,
and I could look inside to my now empty chair.

WEATHER IS BEAUTIFUL

NICOLE CALLIHAN

Maxine, I've been swimming in my husband
the sculpture garden. I run my hands over the prickly
and shoot up for air, marvel at how that becomes this.

K. got an advance to paint the rain,
And D. started "how to contain her," a libretto.
R. is teaching me what to hate about the bourgeoisie.
Me, I'm still knocking around in this body.

Don't even get me started on my mother.
My God, my mother. My mother, my God.

But it's the girls you wouldn't recognize.
I hate to say they bloomed over night
but you know how spring goes. Bloomboomboom.

Last week, my student turned in an essay
in which she proves the soul is real.
It only weighs seven ounces but it is real.
Which is to say: I am nearly half a pound of soul
set off by 130 lbs of fat, sinew and last night's pimento cheese.

My particular collision of particles, though,
is happy (if still concerned about X.

Will I take X to the grave? Will X take me?).
Anyway, sending you the world on this
fairly well-written postcard from Hawaii.
Wish you were not dead but here.

N.

WOODPILE

DEAN P. JOHNSON

The dog chases the wish of a chipmunk
and like the dream, it weaves and dodges,
diving through the wood near where
the old man squats on an upturned
stump used as a slaughtering post
for good solid whole green logs.
The old man grimaces, and, like a good son,
I look away as though lost in the dog's dream
as he digs at the fringe of the woodpile,
runs to one side and then to the other,
snarls, growls, whimpers with frustration.
Smiling at his premature exhaustion,
he lets out a weak "whew."
I turn, force a smile, and comment
on all the work we have done,
only half of what used to be done,
back when I detested these crisp mornings,
smelling exhaust, gas, dead leaves and sawdust,
when I feigned illness just to sleep in,
when I'd say things not knowing what harm
a son can do to a father by saying such things,
when the river between us was wide,
choppy, unnavigable, unbridgeable, green.
I lay the ax on the hard frozen ground

and pick up the scattered splits of wood.
"Don't overdo it," he breathlessly says.
Not to make him feel any worse,
I quickly toss the wood on top of the pile
and kneel down beside the old man
loudly uttering a forced "whew."
As he watched the dog still digging, still sniffing,
still chasing after the hope of his chipmunk,
I watch him: gaunt, emaciated, drawn, unshaven,
unlike when the river between us was wide.
Now, when we can easily leap from bank to bank,
no longer boy to man but man to man,
he is frail so I must carry his work load.
I'd rather hate him than to see him like this:
betrayed by his own body, cancer consumed.
He pulls himself up with the momentum of a second try.
I dare not help him; it's not time for that yet,
but we both know it will come to that soon enough.
He picks up one split of wood and tosses it
onto the woodpile, but the piece falls short,
landing near the dog whose nose has been
sniffing in the gaps for the scent of hope.
Startled, the dog yelps and runs off toward the house.
The old man quickly turns and notices me watching him.
He reaches into his coat, pulls out a cigarette,
lights it, inhales, exhales, coughs, spits,
wipes his mouth with his coat sleeve,
then slowly follows the dog.

MEMORY PALACE

AARON BROWN

Let us implore that it be returned to us,
That second space.
—Milosz

In my father's house, there are rooms where I might wander,
finding in each the rubble of childhood—a reading chair,
maroon rug, cluttered toys—things on which I could
place a memory, if only I could return—

return to search the worn spines of books with talking mice,
to trace Arabic calligraphy with untrained eyes and speak
the words of a language primer: *Ghitatti sakhira, ismaha Samira.*
I could cover these covers with a thought I never wish to lose.

Each room would be a category—in one, the cabinet of drawers
housing a friend who found a gun in his father's car, the car in which
he drove the sheikh, and the father who found his son's blood on the seat.
In my schoolroom, the desk over which the owls clawed in the rafters

where I project the time I hunted with a sling birds the size of my thumb,
and found none. An unstrung bow to remind me of the afternoons
when I couldn't mark the words, couldn't say, *How is your health?*
Will you be back tomorrow? The time I was promised he would return,

but he never did and something was missing from my toys,
a bright green gun. A bright green gun to remind me of the trucks
burdened with soldiers speeding off to the eastern front, leaving
a wake of dust only too eager to rise. And how could I forget

the dust that rests on every countertop and crevice, chair and shoe?
The particles raised by the mortar and pestle beating to the smoke
of cookfires, dust settling on my bed, in a closet, down a hall where
I articulate all memories into one: a toy gun, unstrung bow,

desk with owl feathers, cabinet spilling blood, the spines of books
I never had the time to read. If I lose the way back to this place,
lose it at a wrong turn and into a wrong room, it will not be for lack
of things to stand in place of other things, but for the will to look for
them.

HARD ELBOW

JOHN GREY

I gave love the hard elbow.
I sang songs of pure hate. "May the seas rise up
and swallow California."
And why? Through some deep belief in
the fatality of science? Because the browsing
moose-head told me so?
I'm sleeping beneath the overpass.
I'm bumming my way down a dusty road,
toward the last town, away from the next.
I stop to dirty up my ears. I'm a slacker
with a vulgar turn of phrase.
Or so says the one that my affection humiliated.
I gave love the lecture and hate the reason.
"I love the sun that burns the green grass brown."
I sleep under the tree. Damn, if only I'd fallen out of it.
I buy a third hand car, rust cheap,
On the flat plain, my one desire is to bust a window
with a brick. I burned love with cold fire.
And hate slammed the gate.
"May it rain and rain and rain
and the one ark have a hole in it."
I get a job driving baby carriages to the dumpster.
Or was that squeezing apartments into pulp.
I gave love the astonished look of love.

And all the past due bills I left with hate.
"Earthquake, I'm your lover now.
Let's split this crazy ground in two together."
I come across a pond but I don't walk across it.
I lounge about its wet mossy banks,
three feet or so from paddling water fowl,
wishing my worst looks were stones.
I gave love my best swan-song.
But that's hate the swans are singing.

SACRAMENT

SARAH JANE MILLER

The small mahogany box kept next to my bed
contains an old rosary of wooden crucifixion,
a man's silver quartz wristwatch still ticking,
and a hard pack of USA Lights 100s.

At night, the cigarettes are removed
for examining more often than the rosary.
For him, these were not conversational cigarettes.
Rather, they were smoked in a silence

where each exhale released something
of which he could never truly be rid.
I pull a slender pale stick out,
clumsily light it, and breathe in

each breath my father could have had left.
Inhale. The smoke embodies me.
Only until lungs are filled
to the point of aching, I exhale.

The smoke dissipates but each breath
is always the same as the one before.
The cigarette burns down
to the small nub of filter. It leaves me

exactly with what I had started.
Yet, now the back of my throat tastes
like the scent of his brown corduroy jacket.
It hangs in my closet like a shed skin.

CRACKS

CODY SMITH

Most days round words packed
his mouth. In our younger years,
his gut still welcomed the belt.
Leather. Our name, Smith, in the back.

His voice shook those days he arranged me across
the bed and counted off the times he cracked
the leather against my welted white and red hide.
It shook off the cypresses those mornings we'd ease
out into the breakwater dammed by beavers that
nearly overcame my chest waders—

him hunkered on the other side of the tree,
sitting on a bald gray cypress knot, water
waist high and yelling *shoot em* when
the mallards and gadwalls circled low enough.

His voice shook the shower mist
the Saturday mornings he'd lather up
my ten year old face with goop squirted out
of a ₵.99 can of Barbasol and he'd say,
this is how you square up sideburns.

Aging, he dug holes into the belt to give it and his
expanding stomach a few more years together. And
still his voice shook the days he'd drive my sister
and me from school to his parent's house
on our weeks with him. It shook the walls
of the house he built for us when he taught
me the difference between three-eighths and five-
sixteenths of an inch, and how to spackle cracks smooth.

GARGOYLES

C.J.A.

These old father-figures,
I turned them to stone.

Shrunk them down.

These little pebble-totems,
I hold them in my pocket:

One is bipolar—lost his pills—

One—a naturalist,
hiking and raw—

One is a liar—a collector
of lies—

One a hunter—smoking his kill—

One—is absent—
on a boat somewhere,
or in a photograph;

his shoes are the shoes I wear.

THE WIDOW COMPLEX

GWEN GOODKIN

was carrying a stack of small plastic bowls, different colors: preschool blue, sour apple, artificial grape. Inside one bowl were four unwanted raspberries and, in the others, droplets of water. We adults could have shared from one bowl, but not three preschoolers. No, they had to have their own bowls, each a different color and each called out like a Saturday-night order at a bar. "Green! I want green!" If a child didn't get the color commanded, he would hop in place, heels pounding the floor, fists pumping and we adults would panic—what to do? give in or hold firm?—and the host always gives in, always, because the host is most concerned with showing what a good host. Which, yesterday, was me.

As far as these play dates go, there must be three of us adults at all times, never less. Because I'm the lone man, I can't meet with only one woman. Even the lady whose face was ripped off by a chimp would cause suspicion. Just the term—play date.

We made our way inside from the front yard. One of my wife's friends walked behind me. We were talking in the disjointed way parents who're half-watching kids do—"And so, you think she's ready for kinder-garten—It's Evelyn's turn, Marissa! Let her have the tricycle. You have to share." That pause of silence while Marissa begrudgingly gave up the tricycle she didn't want to play with until she saw Evelyn grab it. "And so, kindergarten. Yeah. Not until she's there socially"—when I felt a spike of pain like an IV needle pushed deep in my thigh.

A couple weeks ago, I opened the mailbox, reached for the pile, felt the stick of threads and pulled my hand back. I lowered to eye level—hers—afraid she would be up front, ready to launch like a flying squirrel. But she was in the back, suddenly awakened by the blast of light, readying her legs—nimble when free of her abdomen's weight—to repair her trap. I thought about killing the widow, but hesitated. As long as she stayed in her corner, what was the harm?

Whenever we're on the swings in the back yard, near the dark wood fence that my wife and I call the Black Widow Condo Complex, I quiz Marissa on spider webs.

"What kind of web is this?" I ask, pointing to one with a pattern, a pretty one.

"A regular spider's," she says. "Not a widow."

"Right," I say. "And that?" I hold my son in the crook of my arm and, with my other hand, I block her from getting too close. I show her quickly what I want her to name, bring my hand back.

"A widow egg sack."

It looks like a dollhouse Chinese lantern made of onionskin with taffy pulls all over. Or a lone barnacle.

"Very good," I say. "And how is a widow's web different from a regular web?"

"A regular web goes round and round. A widow's web goes back and forth. All over." She draws zigzags with her finger, still chubby at the base.

"Or—?"

"Or it's like a sail, except the sail is at the bottom like the trampoline at gymnastics, not straight up."

If I flip over Marissa's tricycle or the plastic car my son sits on to scoot across the sidewalk, between the wheel and axle or under the seat: an empty egg sac, the remnants of an earwig, a skein of disconnected strands waving loose in the breeze. I saw a television show once where a man in Australia shoved his foot into a boot he'd left in his garage and got bit by a huge recluse. The foot necrosed, then he died. Now, if I leave a pair of shoes outside, I give them two good shakes, slap the toe then look into the cave of it. Even then, when I push my foot in—

At Halloween we walked past homes decorated with the usual pumpkins, witches, ghosts. One house had fake webbing stretched across bush branches, no pattern, nearly opaque with random strands.

"What kind of web is that?" I asked Marissa.

"Widow," she said. "Widows are black or brown."

A couple days after the widow wove her trap, I opened the mailbox and saw another spider walking on the side wall, one slow step, one leg at a time, toward her.

"Turn back, buddy," I said. "Bad idea."

Then the next day, I pulled out the mail and there he was, a thin, limp skeleton on top of a credit card offer.

Day after day, I'd see a spider creeping toward the back and the next day, its skeleton would be smashed or wedged or hanging loose in the mail pile. Then she built a web screen around herself to hide behind. Every day, another skeleton, another spider stepping careful to its death. Soon she grew too big for the screen and moved to the opposite corner, no longer concerned about whether they could see her or not. They came anyway.

Once I put my son in his swing out back. It's a bucket swing for a baby, so has leg holes with a strip in the middle to hold him in place. The swing's chain ends in a metal triangle and the bottom of the triangle attaches to the seat through a metal channel like an empty door hinge. Marissa twisted on the swing next to him. He was still young, maybe four months, so I sat in front of him and pushed with my fingertips while I drained a beer.

After he'd been in there for a while, I saw the bunch of white thread at the front of the triangle's channel. I stood, put my beer high, stopped the swing by the chain, lifted him out as if he were a fibula in the game of Operation, set him ten feet away on the grass, told Marissa to get next to him and peered into the channel. She was in there, though I wasn't sure—dead or alive. I found a stick. My hand shook. I stood as far away as I could then stabbed the stick into the empty space.

The spider came out the other end, sprinted across the top, front legs high, challenging me to a duel. Brown recluse. I pulled off my flip flop and slammed it on the swing. The baby cried. Marissa shouted, "Daddy! Dad!" The spider fell to the grass.

"Stay back!" I said. The baby was crying so hard I knew I'd have snot to wipe. Then Marissa. "Dad! Where is it? Daddy! Did you kill it? Dad!"

I lifted my bare foot, hopped then planted it atop my other. I bent to study the grass. Then I saw it, scrambling, hiked front legs, "I'm coming for you, bastard."

I pounded the grass with my shoe, trying to back away, but not able to reach past a certain point, then stopped myself and watched it curl into death.

"Dad! Dad! Did you get it, Dad?"

My previous self had a PhD. I still have the degree, of course, just not the drive to keep up the constant churn of dissection. I acknowledged too late my hatred for literary theory. When I finally stepped away from the pomp and circumstance, I understood that literary theory did to books what gross anatomy did to bodies. I'd come to dread lifting the cover of a new book, which, at one time, had been my favorite feeling in the world. The classes were less a time for debate and discussion and more about title-dropping every book ever written and, more importantly, who could be most clever at kissing the professor's ass. When one professor walked in with his nails manicured, rubbing his thumb back and forth over the uniform edges all through class, it sent me over the edge. Pretense. I thought. The point of the degree isn't academic. It's to prove how far the distance from other men. When, in truth, all men love sex.

My wife is a principal in an advertising agency, which means she's the most stylish person within a ten-mile radius of our suburban desert town. This isn't much of a problem for her since she grew up in New York City, one of the things that drew me—a small-town Ohio guy—to her. It seemed so exotic, growing up in the big city. Then, after a while, I realized kids in a big city end up making their own small town of it, that they drink cheap beer outdoors, too, (in parks, not fields like us country kids) and scuttle away when cops make an appearance.

My wife can make the blandest gray dress look like the most stylish outfit you've ever seen. Maybe it's her—she elevates anything she puts on. Or maybe it's like a college major, something she's studied and perfected over the years. She's always a step ahead of every trend. "For every action, there is an equal and opposite reaction," she says. "All you have to do is look at what's going on now and do the opposite." Then she smiles and says, "The trick is to do it first. But, don't tell anyone. It's the secret ingredient in my style recipe."

What I really fell in love with was her laugh. It's completely free and wild. When she laughs, she's no longer a grown woman, but a girl without responsibility or cares and I get to spend those brief moments with that girl.

My wife might as well get on a plane every day and fly to Istanbul, that's how distant our worlds. Every morning, she showers, dresses, makes herself up, and goes off into the world while I heat bottles, pick up browned banana half-moons from the carpet, offer a snack, change a diaper, push dirty clothes into the washing machine, offer snack, diaper change, push wet clothes into the dryer, preschool, grocery shop, snack, diaper, meal prep, swim class, diaper snack, park trip, doctor visit, diaper snack, control rage as kids throw uneaten dinner at the floor and walls, bath, diaper snack, books, bottle.

Repeat.

When my wife comes home from work, she hugs the kids, every once in a while she hugs me, then she sits at the kitchen table like a ripped squeeze toy, quiet and empty. She is always genuinely appreciative of the dinners I cook, and compliments me on what great food I make, saying she could never do what I do.

Since the bulk of what I do is provide food and wipe clean its remnants, I now wonder if I should have gone to culinary school. Most days my biggest struggle is what would I rather? Stand up, walk out the door and never once look back or drop neck-first from the doorframe.

Every other month when a huge deal is closing, she works weekends, too. By the second Sunday, I'm at cliff's edge and I haul the kids to the pizza joint where Marissa runs squealing between the long wooden tables, annoying everyone who doesn't have a young child in tow. My son sits on my thigh, staring at the blinking lights of video games and I drink a pint. Without fail, some woman will approach me and say one of the following:

1. "You teach jui-jitsu at Westside Martial Arts, right? I see you through the window on Tuesday mornings before my bikram yoga class."
2. "Oh my God, you're the early morning weatherman. Can we take a picture with you?" (Because nothing makes some women more uncomfortable than a man without a job, so they just go ahead and assign me one.)
3. "Daddy Day Care today, huh? Letting Mom have a break?" Then gives me a smile normally reserved for a young child and may even go so far as to pat my upper arm.

About the forty-first time #3 came around, I looked at the woman dead serious and said, "I normally never help, I mean raising kids is a woman's job, right? But she's on the rag today, so here we are." and I finished the last half of my beer as the woman stood there staring, gape-mouthed, then I winked, raised my glass and said "Cheers."

Of course, there's the other end of the spectrum where I get the long end of the stick and all the credit for being a great parent. A lone man with two kids in the grocery store will get no less than five "atta boys" between the milk aisle and the checkout stand.

Whereas, the way my wife tells it, a mother hears how beautiful or cute or well-behaved her kids. Never a compliment to her. Because what else is there to her? As if by bearing a child her own body has ceased to exist and has nothing more to offer the world.

My wife's body is what I saw first when we met. It was perfectly hour-glass and she knew how to show it off without showing too much. After two kids, she still looks damn good, more like a woman, but she doesn't see it that way and, consequently, I don't see it much anymore, let alone touch it.

She has these strange feminist ideas about how my cupping her breast or grabbing her ass is treating her like an object, but really, I just want to be close to her and feel the warmth that was so easy and uncomplicated before we brought two other people into our relationship. She says I'm trying to put her in her place, to assert my power over her because of the situation I'm in, how powerless I can sometimes feel about my own life.

Who knows, maybe she's right. But in the moment when I reach for her, I can say with all honesty, I'm not thinking of anything but her naked body.

One night in bed, she was reading W Magazine, which is the size of legal paper, but wider. Basically, she needs a music stand to read the monster so her arms don't get tired. She dropped the magazine to her lap and said, "Jeff Pardo is getting divorced for the second time."

She broke the quiet right as I was falling asleep, so I answered with a "Hmmm."

"He said his first divorce was easier, even though they had kids. They were both reasonable, and, in the end, just friends who grew apart. They worked out the custody agreement without any drama. The money. All that." She picked up the magazine again. "The second wife, he says, wants everything she can get. And they were only married two years."

I was awake by then and pushed a hand under my head. "I suppose if that happened with us, I'd move out and get an apartment. You could keep the house."

"No," she said and flipped a page. "We'd sell the house and split it."

And it bothered me how fast she responded, how she had an answer ready.

The hardest part of being a full-time dad is that dudes only get together to do something. So, even though I know other guys in the same boat as me, we don't meet up much. Unless we're riding a bike or playing racquetball, climbing, skateboarding, dribbling a soccer ball, basketball, throwing a football, golfing, swinging a bat, essentially anything that involves a ball—we aren't spending an afternoon together. A friend and I tried tennis once because at least the kids were contained in the court, but a lob to a tiny shoulder blade put an end to the match. Not to mention it was summer—bad idea, even if the court's shaded. Walk outside in the summer and the heat is an instant headache that slowly drains a body's energy one sweat drip at a time.

And then I think friendships are too complicated at this age. I'm happy just hanging out with my kids. They're my best friends and, really, who needs more than two friends? The kids and I get a cup of ice cream and sit on a bench in the shade to people watch. My daughter next to me, holding her plastic spoon with a pinky lifted, which fascinates me because it isn't learned. The pinky lift must be tied to a specific gene on the female DNA. And then there's my boy with his spoon in his fist. Marissa taking careful bites and my son with those wide-spaced teeth toddlers have, ice cream like a goatee and we're quiet, just eating, and every once in a while my son will say "puppy" or "Hi!" to a passing airplane and, in between, his sounds of contentment, which are different than babbling, somewhere between singing and talking. Babbling is practice talk, loud and precise. Sounds of contentment are more like pigeon coos, half sound, half air. Then my daughter wipes the corners of her mouth and lifts her ice cream cup with her thumb and middle finger and drops it in the trash. She leans into my free leg and drops her head against my ribs and I'm hers and she's mine. And I know then I'll never leave her. It is she who will leave me.

The dregs of the day, 5-8 pm—those are the hardest. That's when I look at the clock every four minutes and wonder if bedtime will ever arrive. And, as I was carrying the kids' stack of bowls, we were up against the dregs, which is why the play dates, to distract us all from "How long 'til bed?"

I felt the needle pierce of pain, and my mind went black for a nano-second, as if a movie were starting, and then it was all there—the mail-box, the skeletons, the webs, the papery egg sacs, the swing, the tricycle, the shoes, The Black Widow Condo Complex. I pitched the bowls, beat my own thigh, the bowls ricocheted off the house and my wife's friends shouted "What! What is it?" and my back hit the ground, my son crying, the preschoolers too scared to speak and I yelled, "Where is it? Where? Do you see?" still slapping my leg and finally I calmed down and Karen spotted a lump of brown on the cement. She moved close and said, "It's a bee." I saw it wasn't moving, that I must have killed it mid-apeshit. My head fell back and I remembered that, soon after she came out of hid-ing and moved to the opposite side of the mailbox, the spiders stopped coming. A couple days later, I searched for her in the dark corner with a strange hope one reserves for the underdog. I figured she could kick open the mailbox with a single leg by then, that she'd probably left for a bigger place with a view. The image of her made me close my eyes and lift my face to the sun's heat and laugh. But I peered in again and found her. I stared for a few moments, waiting for movement, but she hung limp— dead from starvation.

LIEBEN, XIII – 379, BY RILKE (1875-1926)

Translated from the German by Owen Lucas

Already the day was dying.
                    The woods were otherworldly.
Bullocks stood among blooming cyclamen,

Under ranks of tall dark firs
                    That a fragrant wind blew.
You were dozing, tired from the road.

I spoke your name, softly:
                    From your white heartseed
A force of ecstasy broke, and a firelily rose.

The evening was red,
                    And your mouth so red,
And so warm, where my lips found it,

The flames passed through us,
                    And would climb the walls
And bring the house to ashes—

The wood was silent. The day had passed.
             A ghost had risen to us,
Had purged the daylight and our want.

The great moon alighted on our hilltop.
Our peace stepped to shore
             From a white boat.

TRENY #7 (ON THE DEATH OF HIS DAUGHTER, URSZULA)

BY JAN KOCHANOWSKI (1530-1584)

Translated from the Polish by Leonard Kress

Hangers draped with clothes you'll never wear;
they miss the warm touch of your body. Moths
will soon begin to feed upon that cloth;
what rhetoric will persuade me now to clear
your closet out? The iron sleeps beside
the starch, ribbons remain wrinkled and knotted
under the golden clasp ... Flowers on your dress, potted
in the fabric of our grief, bloom since you died.

Useless flowered garments, they should be boxed
and given to the poor. I fear we've lost
too much in boxing you instead, this crate
shipped off to Hades, its cargo—my fate.
For I've just sealed this oak chest's heavy lid,
forever shutting away the dowry and the bride.

WAR

HEDD WYN (ELLIS EVANS, 1887-1917)

Translated from the Welsh by Michael Ratcliffe

Woe that I live in such a morose age.
God ebbs on the far horizon.
After Him, Man, both king and commoner,
Raises his ugly authority.

When he felt God going away,
He raised a sword to kill his brother.
The sound of battle is in our ears,
Its shadow is on poor cottages.

The old harps formerly borne,
Are hung on yon willow branches.
The screams of boys fill the wind
And their blood mixes with the rain.

2015

MY FATHER CALLED THE MOURNING DOVES

NANCY ALLEN

and I thought they answered him.
Sitting at the kitchen table
beside a screened window,
humid Virginia summers,
the fan thrumming and clicking
in its rounds. Didn't he show me
a thousand times how to cup
my hands just so, to blow
through the space at the base
of the thumbs, to press together
my fingers and wave them quick,
as one, to make the sad echo
that all the mourning doves
all around heard, and hearkened to?
Didn't the sky fill then
with the song of mourning doves
calling to my father?

2016

MASSAGE SONNET

JEN KARETNICK

AT MANDARA SPA, ARUBA MARRIOTT,
REMEMBERING DEBORAH DIGGES

Offer yourself in the way of a child,
splayed and unconcerned about the curl
of a limb, the arrangement of towel
revealing the shell of shy genital.
The hands that wave and recede deal with parts,
oiling rusty mechanisms. Submit.
Allow your mouth to drool. Show all your warts.
This is the hour your best poems will visit,
and your worst. Later, you can only rescue
so many words but some will be enough
to compensate for this half-conscious theft.
Do only what you have been told to do:
Relax your arm; roll over; focus your breath.
So much, or so little, time might be left.

STILL FINDING YOUR HAIR IN MY CLEAN LAUNDRY

FM STRINGER

White beach in the fog on Christmas Eve

Smudge moon, waveless pale sea, salt on air

And tongue, plunge of breast I will not again

Mouth, proud cat toying with a dead bird

Proud clean sheets pulled taut for no one

Tongue on salt pebbled skin, spoon to saucer

Rising through wind, sea fleck and time

Shining belly, tuft of golden tangle, voice

A silver balloon flushing with lift, morning

Moon-face, dream-face, hazing over ...

O beautiful swimmer in the soft distance

No telling if you're really there

Coming back to shore, drifting out to sea

WITH THE DOG AT BERNHEIM FOREST

CLARE BANKS

We walked the field where the path edged
the trees, spindly stands of cedar at first,
then oaks, chestnut—their numbers,
I could see, farther in, shut out even

the dim, winter light. My father whistled
something bright and clear in the cold
as I stayed close, matching my stride to his.
The dog ran in and out of the woods thrilled

and trembling—there was life ranging
in the bracken and she was off her leash.
Eyeing the fallen needles and leaves,
she must have caught the rabbit's scent

or she saw something flicker, as an eye
might—a shock of white on its breast.
A ridge of fur bristled along her spine
and she stopped dead for a moment,

then ran. We watched her dodge trees,
leap over downed branches, the sound

of her chase fracturing the air.
She must have caught it by the neck.

And then, her low, guttering growl.
My father took the rabbit from her mouth
and laid it in his hat. We'll bring it home,
he said. We'll bury it in the lilies.

LATE RAIN

ROY BENTLEY

1. The Light from a Woman's Hair

Some part halos the indentation on the pillow;
some approximates after-sleep's last placement;
another is the eye-numbing white of sheet.

A fraction arrives as through Heaven's window
to vibrate the world-outside strings of a windchime.
A slender-limbed woman transforms the half-visible

before the cheap motel room mirror, works
to loose a particularly knotted length of hair.
The knot isn't her life; the knot is a knot—

but connected to everyone except herself,
islanded in brightness, she is what is called
lovely: shawled in white and white-gold.

2. It

It's a matter of taking hold of one hand
and letting go another, if you're lucky,
though everyone but you knows how desperate

and sees through talk of affection's sea change
as through a fine screen. Still, seeing through
a white puff of winter breath isn't breathing,
which is to say that any set of disappointments
shared is a relationship, the big It, as in
It was all I could do not to tell her the truth.
When it's the case of needing to be released
to someone else's keeping, it's not easy—
because it's you who wants this for what it isn't.

It hardly has to do with wanting anymore.
It really is out of your hands, isn't it?

3. Late Rain

Adultery is like putting down a dog:
the thing is, it has to be done,
though it's brutish work and called for
since what won't fix won't heal, either.

The test of inviolate love is multiple choice;
that whispering in the ear says what happens
happens for good; and your job is to still
the animal within a mostly sterile field.

In some countries, the penalty is death
and death licks a pair of faces like a cat.
To think they imagined a better life wherein
an ordinary voice was bread out of nowhere

in the way anything fine is sudden, beautiful.
On the radio a man sang *Gone*, pure twangy country,
in the office of memory where late rain gentles.
Bill me, you said because it wasn't free.

4. Buying a Handgun in Late March

The guy behind the counter at the gun store
calls the brass jacketed hollow-point ammunition
"man stoppers." Says they're for home protection,
though the truth is they'll compromise body armor.
He sells me a box of twenty-five. The cartridges
are for the Colt Gold Cup Trophy Model .45
matched to a Galco leather shoulder holster.
What's wrong with this picture is what's wrong
with love; there's no waiting period, no talk of
responsibility or wounds you can't be saved from.

What the guy should have said is *It's time to decide*
if this is an act of faith or a surrender. Which is it?
What he doesn't say waits in the overwhelming
Ohio air like a leaf bud as much buried in itself
as the sheath it breaks free of with a violence.

THE SEXINESS OF OLDER PEOPLE

ROY BENTLEY

Why not every joy-toy and thingamajig imaginable,
meaning what's pleasing or acceptable to the rookie

is perfected by hands examining a plural happiness.
Antediluvian Clark Gable can bed Marilyn Monroe,

even with leg tremors and having to start stop start,
cracking his major-movie-star smile at who we are

and what we thought on the way to boundlessness.
Maybe it's the allusion to movies, but I'm thinking

about the quantum mechanics of starlight-as-DNA,
a chemistry of doggedness, but that isn't it exactly.

I'm thinking of my aunt touching my dead uncle.
He was her husband. I was about to say *her friend*.

A drape of bunting bellying around the catafalque
below a casket a Holiness preacher had pounded—

I remember she leaned over in an act of defense
as if what this is about is protecting one another.

2016

How else to say *Goodbye* after years of sweet sex
and the pleasures of falling asleep together after?

EEL FISHING, LEAHI BEACH

LOREN MORENO

Could I ever convince you to go back
to that night sitting on the rock wall jutting out
into the Pacific? Diamond Head's old man face
watching us wait forever for tugs on our line,

a signal that we've caught that elusive lightning
hidden away in the crevices of the rocks.
A summer sky blends into water.
Beneath us tiny phosphorescent fish,

with their night vision, make their way
to the edge of the Earth, back to the constellations.
We eat cherries, spitting out poison-filled pits.
Turning our faces toward the mists off the ocean,
we talk about everything but—

God dials down the knob on the night
and the stars brighten. Then a jingle bell signal:
We finally catch one, its skinny whirling dervish dance
all silvers and greens. Contain it to a bag and hang

it from the rocks. We strip the clothes off
our bodies, jumping into the water. A rush

2016

of ripples surges out across the sea,
our message, unbottled, to a bedridden world.

The bag on the rocks it's wriggling, violently,
as if it contains a million moaning stars. The eel,
restless in its captivity, eventually reels
itself free
(and after all that waiting).
We intended to let it go, though, didn't we?
But what else did we lose, without meaning to?

2017

THE YEAR SHE LIVED ON THE BUS

MARGARET ADAMS

In 2016, she lived on the bus. It was an odd year, despite the predictable paths her home carved through the city, always late for the rush-hour stops on the west side and often early at the beginning of the route, occasionally missing traffic lights on purpose. The temperature was better regulated than she could remember it ever being in any of her prior homes, except on those days when she sat too close to the middle doors, which would bring in a flash of the outside world when they opened and floods of air that gusted whenever more than six people were boarding or exiting at a time. She was always in motion and yet she stayed within the same thirty-six rows of seats, holding still while landmarks rocketed by.

By the eighth month of her residence on the bus, she had begun to figure that something was wrong and think that maybe she should find a new place to live. But deceleration, as she had begun to imagine it, felt like both solution and requisite for finding solution. Instead, she was lulled by the steady thrum of the bus's engine as it traced the roadways, the jouncing rattle of the glass window cool against her forehead. Weeks flicked by with the bus stops.

When at last she packed up her things—she had spread over several seats in the back row by then, claiming extra square footage for her coffee maker and her books—and began to consider cross-streets with an eye towards picking her egress, the bus, sensing her disloyalty, rebelled. It blew past some stops altogether, or opened and closed the doors for a fraction of the necessary time, leaving would-be passengers stranded and indignant. She had visions of the bus crashing, running out of gas, of having to kick out the emergency exit before disappearing into a down-town crowd. In the end, though, it came down to this: her hanging on to the stop cord, her whole weight suspended, not sure if she was struggling to force the bus to halt or refusing to let it go.

When the bus wheezed to a stop at last, she released the handholds and tripped down the steps outside. The doors hissed shut behind her, with no more fanfare or finality than they'd had for any other passenger who had come and gone in the last year. It heaved itself off of the curb with an asthmatic whine and continued its arc around the city. Gone.

She stood. She waited, for a moment, but nothing around her shifted. She realized that to find her next home, she would have to move herself. She hefted her backpack, and walked.

THE FLASHER

JAIME FOUNTAINE

That was the summer that the guy drove around showing girls his dick. He wore a ski mask so he could look you in the eyes while he was doing it, in just a t-shirt and basketball shorts, like a burglar going to the gym.

The news made it out like there was a dangerous predator on the loose, but he never got out of the car, never touched anyone. We mostly just thought it was funny. He'd drive up to you with it flopped over his shorts, not even hard or anything.

Lauren saw it first. "Is that what they really look like?" She asked. "Was that normal?" Lauren has two sisters. Her dad is one of those guys who keeps his shoes on in the house.

"Why would you go up to the car?" Emily has the earliest curfew. Her oldest brother joined the army after graduation last year when he knocked up his girlfriend.

"I never saw one before," Lauren said. "I was curious."

***

The first time I saw him, he had his pants on. I don't know how I knew. I just did.

He was working the register at the convenience store where we'd gone with a Ziploc bag of change we'd scrounged from our couches and our parents' cars to buy Icees. I always mixed the blue raspberry and the coke ones together. It turned my tongue a dark bruise purple, almost black, and no one ever asked to share.

We were trying to be polite about paying with change, counting it out ahead of time, knowing how much the tax would be, but he still looked at us like we were assholes.

He wasn't a teenager, but he wasn't that old. He was skinny in the way that a lot of guys are before they get fat, a month-old buzz cut, some zits. He wasn't special. Maybe if you got to know him.

"What are you looking at?" he asked.

"Nothing," I said.

If you stare at a man and don't break eye contact, a grown one especially, it makes them nervous. There's nothing a man can do to you for looking at him that way. Not in front of people.

"Well, stop," he said, but I didn't. I just smiled as I slid the pile of nickels and dimes toward him.

"I bet he's the flasher," I said.

"Ewwwww. No. "

"I hope it's my brother's friend Eric. He's really cute."

"You're not supposed to have a crush on the flasher."

"But I don't want to see some stranger's dick!"

"That's the whole point. You're not supposed to want it. "

* * *

The next time I saw him, he wasn't working, just stopping by the store, and I couldn't tell if he looked worse or better for it. Probably the same. He had on basketball shorts, which was a sign.
He rustled in and out, keys in hand, clutching his paycheck. I was sitting on the curb, waiting for Emily.

"I know it's you." He turned around, and I could feel his eyes on me, but I knew better than to look up. I just acted like the rocks in the parking lot were the most interesting things in the world until he got into his car and drove away.

* * *

Friday night, I was babysitting until almost 11, so I missed seeing him in action. Two girls on my block saw him and ran off screaming.

"I just saw the mask. I didn't even look down."

"Sure you didn't." The boys in my neighborhood are more obsessed with this guy than we are. They're used to being included. I think they're jealous.

"I didn't! That way if my mom asks, I'm not lying. I don't want to get trapped inside all summer just because some guy can't keep it in his shorts."

She was right. There was no sense in getting punished for someone else's bad behavior.

* * *

I had a hard time convincing anyone that I was right about the flasher, but when he was working, no one else wanted to go to the counter. Lauren, who seemed a little too interested, figured out his schedule, so we stopped going on Monday, Wednesday, and Thursday afternoons, or Saturday mornings.

At least, as a group. I still had to go sometimes for my mom, if we ran out of milk or whatever. She hated going grocery shopping, and something is always better than nothing.

* * *

One Saturday, I walked over when she was still sleeping with five dollars from her purse for milk, and maybe some donuts, if I planned it right.

He was at the register, shuffling the newspapers around, trying not to make eye contact when I got to the counter. I stared at him until he did.

"What's your problem?"

"I don't have one."

"You have a staring problem."

I thought for a second about telling him that I knew who he was and what he was doing, or yelling, "flasher!" in the store. But who would believe me?

I reached into the racks beneath the counter and took a Mounds bar. Confident, though it wasn't what I wanted. I pulled the seam of the plastic, shoved in a bite, daring him to charge me, never breaking eye contact. But he didn't. He didn't say a word

He watched me eat that candy bar, that sweaty slab of sunscreen-flavored soap, in three bites. And he put my milk in the bag next to that little box of powdered donuts, and he let me walk away.

KNOWN FACTS ABOUT GOD

TEMIM FRUCHTER

Technically, she loved Moshe Ber. At least her eyes went swimmy when she thought of him or when anyone else said his name. He went to the boys' school in Baltimore. After meeting him at the big Orthodox youth weekend, she wrote him a painstaking note, two whole sides of looseleaf paper, with little o's on top of the i's like she saw girls do on television when they were trying to be exceptionally girly. Seventh grade and already she was a deft suitor, strung the words together like a song. She gave her heart fast and full, understood she might well be a consummate lover before she understood geometry or her own body. She gave the note to Shira Ziskind, who lived in Pikesville, and who sometimes talked to boys on the weekends.

She waited. Most days after school she closed the door of her small room and lay on the small bed listening to Ricky Nelson or The Beatles and imagining the feel of the exact edge of someone else's lips on her own. Sometimes she was so overcome by waiting that her body started shaking. She'd have to crawl under the covers then, which sometimes helped, even though cold wasn't at all what she was. Sometimes she prayed, but she never opened her mouth to do it.

Here was what she knew about God: God didn't want women eating messy sandwiches in public, because it was immodest. God also didn't want you writing out the name God like it was a full name. You wrote God like G-d, which confused her, because who was anything but affirmed by the sight of their own full name? God didn't want people kissing other people or having any weird kinds of sex. Maybe any kinds of sex at all. And the only kinds of people allowed to have the non-weird sex were men and women who were married to each other. God had a green beard, like the framed painting of the stern-looking hasid in her grandmother's living room. God wasn't particularly handsome, nor was he particularly old, but he was square-shaped and you listened. Of course he was a he. Mostly written as He, except if by secular authors, witches, or heretics.

The night Moshe Ber called her she wasn't expecting it, though she noticed she wasn't entirely surprised. The phone was for her, her mother called upstairs. She wriggled out from under the covers and picked it up like she hadn't willed it to ring. I got your number from Shira Ziskind, he said. He told her that he had liked her note, especially the weird story at the end about the invention of the pickle, and had been working on a pictorial response that he would send with Shira the next time he saw her. She held her breath the whole time he was talking. His voice was deeper than she remembered. He told her he was pretty good at comics and was learning electric bass. She noticed that Moshe Ber didn't ask her any questions, except at the end, when he asked her if she was going to the next Orthodox youth weekend, and would they see each other soon?

She felt the receiver sticky on her cheek. How long had they been talking? Had she spoken at all? What did her legs look like? They chafed under her skirt most of the time and sometimes she forgot them. She remembered them now because she felt them shaking, and couldn't tell whether this was voluntary. She wanted something big to happen, like a pompadour. Did Moshe Ber have a pompadour? She couldn't picture him now. Did he know how to dance? What did dancing feel like? She didn't love the feeling of holding her breath, she had to admit.

I don't think I'm going to go. The words were rogue, out of her mouth before she could reconsider. Too much homework, as if that was something. She felt like crying suddenly, zero to sixty, hoped his quiet meant they'd somehow gotten disconnected. She closed her eyes and imagined one day touching a curve, someone else's wishing skin. She pictured God like she did sometimes, except with soft fingers and a mess of curly hair. It made her gasp. She wished the phone back into its cradle so that she could just be still again. So she would wait. She would wait for a pompadour.

Maybe she would be the pompadour. She would learn to dance one day. She had gotten pretty excellent at waiting.

Pause pause. But I'm excited to see your note. And oh. That there. Saying excited out loud just then felt like a dare, like remembering her legs, or like God's entire face blowing open.

WORD SEARCH

MICHELE FINN JOHNSON

1. It shouldn't be so hard to say hello. That's the whole point of the word, right? To break the ice?

2. Urban legend has it that Alexander Graham Bell coined the "hello" greeting during the world's first telephone call to his girlfriend, Margaret Hello. I guess he was looking for something to say once she picked up. Hello? I imagine him asking. Margaret Hello? Is that you? As if someone else could have possibly been on the other end.

3. When I call you, you don't answer. Or you answer, but then you hear my voice, "Hello? Hello?" And then I hear, click.

4. The word "hello" is actually an alteration of "hallo," which itself is an alteration of "holla" and "hollo," all of which were 1800s shouts used to attract attention, kind of like "Yoo hoo" or "Hey there!"

5. Now that I think of it, your first words to me were "Hey there." When I looked up and saw you, your Italian horn necklace, Jack and Coke fizzing with lime, I wanted to bolt. I thought I knew your whole story in those first seconds—West Philly, Madonna statue on the front lawn, chest hair for days. I couldn't have known it all, though. I couldn't have guessed.

6. The fact is, Alexander Graham Bell insisted that the word "Ahoy" be used as the primary telephone greeting. By 1900, he lost out to his rival, Thomas Edison, and the word "hello." But Bell felt so strongly about "ahoy" that he used it for the rest of his life.

7. We sat barefoot, cross-legged on your front lawn, the plastic Madonna statue behind us. We devoured an entire bag of Chips Ahoy while Fourth of July fireworks blasted from city rooftops. Later that night— our first time. You loomed above me in bed and I saw it, too late to ask—the inky name engraved on your bicep. Lucille.

8. Mabel Hubbard was Alexander Graham Bell's girlfriend, not Margaret Hello. So the urban legend is false, unless Alex was two-timing poor Mabel? Seems unlikely that a man who championed the word "ahoy" would be the cheating type.

9. Maybe if you'd been my winter boyfriend—long sleeves, dark nights. But you romanced me with summer snow cones, weekends in Ocean City. Lucille exposed by concert tees; Lucille covered in sand and surf bubbles. Lucille, the other woman, the temptress with the name of a geriatric librarian.

10. If you answer the phone and ask me to defend myself, I'll say Lucille drove me crazy. I mean—Hello! Hallo! Holla! Hollo! You refused to explain.

11. I force myself to remember. That night I traced the loops of Lucille's 'L's' with my fingers while you slept; that night you swatted my hand away; that morning you left early for work and told me to stay, to sleep in, to hang out; that day I opened all of your drawers, cabinets, boxes until I found the photo albums; that photo that's so obviously you and Lucille, labeled "Halloween 1997"; that cowboy hat that dwarfs your head and squashes your curls; that Patsy Cline hair flip that frames Lucille's heart-shaped face; those bangs that highlight Lucille's moon-eyes, those eyes aimed only at you.

12. The mid-19th century British word "hullo" is deceptive. It was not used as a greeting, but rather an expression of surprise, as in "Hullo, what have we here?"

13. You use a more slang-y version of "Hullo, what have we here?" when you surprise me and come home early; dozens of Lucille photos litter your bedroom floor.

14. According to the American Heritage Dictionary, "hallo" is a modification of the obsolete "holla," as in Stop!

15. When you shout, the veins in your neck seem to stretch beyond the limits of your skin.

16. Lucille is dead. Lucille is dead. Lucille is dead.

17. The Italian word "ciao" is used for both hello and goodbye. Other words with this dual meaning: "shalom" in Hebrew, "salaam" in Arabic, "annyeong" in Korean, "aloha" in Hawaiian.

18. The last things I remember: you saying that we were only a slim beat away from being something, a slim beat, a slim beat; tear streaks on your bulging neck; words no longer words; the slick surface of Polaroids on the bottoms of my feet.

19. You will not answer the phone. You will not say hello or goodbye; ahoy or ciao. It shouldn't be this hard, but it is.

WHAT A HEADLESS BOY WOULD SEE

CATHY ULRICH

Somebody died at the carnival that night. We saw the lights go out on the rides, bit by bit. Mona's brother had been there. He said some kid lost his arm on the Scrambler.

Or his head, I don't know, said Mona's brother.

Lost something, anyway, he said, made a slashing motion across his throat with one hand.

From Mona's house, we could see the lights at the carnival were still out. She kicked her feet on the rocking swing on the front porch, chewed the side of her thumb.

We should go, she said.

* * *

Mona was that girl in school the other girls hated. Wore cheap eyeshadow and had a gap in her teeth, the curliest hair any of us had ever seen. I was always going over to her house. It didn't matter. The other girls hated me too.

* * *

Mona had fingers like spiders, crawled them over my shoulders. She was braiding my hair when the lights at the carnival went out, left me with a half-finished French braid.

Huh, she said.

The lights, she said.

She liked my hair, how soft it was, how it always smelled nice. Her fingers went up and down my shoulders. I shivered and laughed.

Okay, she said. I'll paint your toenails.

* * *

I was staying over at Mona's that night. She kept putting me in her clothes that were too small but too nice for just getting rid of, spreading her bluest shadow across my eyelids. I held still, so still, while she ran the brush over my skin.

Her brother was in his bedroom, texting his friends about the kid that died.

We waited for the sound of her parents' sleep breath. She put me into the prom dress she'd worn at her old school, where she'd been dating a senior — older man, she laughed, her words tickling the back of my neck. She spun me round to face the mirror on the back of her bedroom door.

She said: Pretty, gave me a kiss on the cheek, left a lipstick smudge.

* * *

She let me wear her best old jeans when we tiptoed out the back door, my oversized tee-shirt draped to my knees.

Letty, she said. Tuck that in. Always called me Letty, which I liked better than Leticia anyway.

I tucked my shirt into the waist of her old jeans.

You look like a cute balloon.

* * *

The carnival wasn't that far from Mona's house. She held my hand while we walked, called me clumsy in the voice like my mother used to call me sweetheart.

You'd trip over the curb or something without me, said Mona. Get run over.

She said: Squish. That would be it for you, squeezed my hand.

* * *

The gate at the carnival was locked. Mona said she would climb, liked to climb. Before our graduation, she would climb the water tower near the school, fall from the tallest rung, or jump. Would lie ragdoll in the field till she was found.

That hadn't happened yet. It was the night somebody died at the carnival. We were at the carnival gate.

Mona was real and dark and alive, held my hand, called me pretty, called me clumsy. In a voice like she really meant sweetheart, honey, love.

You stay here, she said. We'll figure out some way to get you in.

* * *

What she wanted was to see the blood, the mess.

They can't have cleaned it all up yet, right?

She wanted to lie down under the Scrambler, look up at the sky, pretend to see what the dying kid saw.

If it was his arm, anyway.

If it was his head?

He probably just saw the ground.

* * *

Mona climbed over the gate like nothing. She looked back at me from the top.

I don't think there's another way in, she said. You have to climb.

I said: No.

I said: No, no, no.

I know you're afraid, said Mona. She reached for me. Her fingernail polish was a pink that wanted to be red.

2017

I'll go without you, she said finally, balanced atop the gate like a glorious raven.

I know, I said. I'll wait for you, sat down in the gravel outside the gate, traced her name in it. Mona, Mona, Mona.

She was already gone. She was already on the ground under the Scrambler, lying wet on her back where they had hosed the blood away, water puddled in the uneven pavement. She was looking up at the sky, said to me when she came back: It was beautiful.

Said: You can't imagine how beautiful it was.

PARK

LAURIE STONE

Park

A woman passed with red toe nails, and they reminded me of my sister. My sister was the person I got along with best. The relationship was like a chest rising up and down. Mozart said writing music was not easy for him. He studied other composers and worked hard on every score. One day my sister could not sit up, although she had been able to sit up the day before. The speed of her decline seemed miraculous, the way it had seemed miraculous for a body to work at all.

A rat ran out from under the bench where I was sitting and darted into the street. It was large and its tail was long and held aloft. In a flash it was gone, the wrong animal in the wrong place, but not to me. It was furtive by nature and maybe experience. I liked being surprised.

When my sister was dying, I loved her as I had always loved her, or more because she was facing the end of her life. I slipped back to being in the family, and there was nothing she could do to help me. Sadness is a museum of sadness. Happiness has no history.

My mother would reach out to my dog. The dog was always wanting to be petted. Usually my mother was afraid of dogs, and maybe she was afraid of this dog, but something in her rose up over her fear, and she petted the dog's head. I was thirty and brought the dog to the city. We went to Central Park and played on the grass. The dog had a black head and a white body. I carried him in a canvas tote. "He's so beautiful," she said again and again, and I wondered if she was imagining a child of mine.

"You're the dog's grandmother," I said. She said, "I'm the grandmother of a dog." A softness came into her eyes. I forgave her for loving my sister more.

One day in Washington Square Park, I came upon a troupe of acrobats performing on the paths. They were dirty and ragged and very beautiful in their feats of juggling and balance. What I liked especially was their indifference to the rest of us who watched with awe. You could see they were having sex with each other, falling into fits of jealousy, then joining the group for dinner. Their talent was larger than they were, and besides they were part of a family. You could see why we wait until almost there is no air.

Thin Man

I would meet the thin man in a Russian bar, where I did not understand the menu. One night he came a long way, and I let him twist. I don't remember why I was pissed. Another night, the last night, I waited for him, imagining his sad eyes searching the dim light. Once night at the bar, I said, "My mother thought children came into the world like tiny cars with motors running and maps laid out." He smiled softly and said, "I don't see my mother much, anymore." I thought I should be careful with him. He had the broad, Australian accent of former criminals. He was smaller and thinner than me, and I liked having sex with him. I don't remember much more than our odd, thin sex and the last night, when he did not come. I kept looking at the door as people swept in like fish. When I realized he wasn't coming, the air took on the bruised color of eggplant, glossy with muscle, and I did not leave.

REALISM

BEN GUNSBERG

When frost becomes plausible as frost
along power lines, I think hard bread
and mottled salami, scrape shit off
my son's crib. Grout tile, caulk sink,
lean back against a brick wall,
blue haze rising off my cigarette.
When objects descend as Brouwer
has shown, paint resembles actual
basements, Thursdays, fathers living
or dead. I stand eight hours, stuffing
circuits into plastic, warned not to
touch my eyes without showering first,
plunge wood in lacquer and scour
the mess with bristling solvent, earn
$8.50 shoveling sawdust into burlap,
reach for the white envelope of credit
that follows apartment to apartment.
I stir the sloshing contents of a pot,
spoon milk-soaked oats into my son's
mouth, wipe his chin with my sleeve,
step over trash littering the doorway,
down the staircase, new syringe,
old jacket pocket.

2018

LIFECOLOR INDOOR LATEX PAINTS – WHITES AND REDS

KRISTEN PLOETZ

Whites

Arrival
Hospital Light – AR101
Doctor's Coat – AR102
Swaddle – AR103
Midnight Feed – AR104
Nonna's Smile – AR105

First Year
Burp Cloth – FY201
First Tooth – FY202
Lost Lamby – FY203
Slice of Moon – FY204
Birthday Cake – FY205

Childhood
Sidewalk Chalk – CH301
Undertow (formerly Riptide) – CH302
Dandelion Fuzz – CH303
Broken Femur – CH304
Vanilla Cone – CH305

2018

Adolescence
32AA – AD401
All-Star Laces – AD402
Mother's Best Sheets – AD403
Bleach – AD404
Levonorgestrel 0.75mg (formerly Morning After) – AD405

Young Adult I
Favorite T-Shirt –YA501
Beer Foam – YA502
Piña Colada – YA503
Benzoylmethylecgonine – YA504
Academic Dismissal – YA505

Young Adult II
Escitalopram 10 mg – YA506
Whitecaps – YA507
Full Dress Whites – YA508
Honorable Discharge – YA509
Size 10 Envelope – YA510

Middle Age
Latte (formerly Waitress Apron) – MA601
Rolling Papers – MA602
Lab Results – MA603
Silicone (Textured) – MA604
Jib Sail – MA605

Senior Years
Empty Pillow – SY701
Bichon Frise – SY702
Broken Hip – SY703
Windowpane – SY704
Soup of the Day – SY705

Departure
Sissy's Handkerchief – DE801
Hospital Blanket – DE802
Knuckles – DE803
Nurse's Sleeve – DE804
Clock Face – DE805

Reds

Learn
Gumball – LN101
Cardinal – LN102
Lost Balloon – LN103
Bicycle – LN104
Skinned Knee – LN105

Live + Leap
Drugstore Valentine – LI201
Menarche – LI202
Rum Punch – LI203
First Bite (formerly Hickey) – LI204
Popped Cherry – LI205

Love
Heart-Shaped Box – LV301
Matching Tattoos – LV302
Push-Up Bra – LV303
Poppy Bouquet – LV304
Dog-Eared Dostoevsky – LV305

Lose
Beer Pong Cup – LS401
2009 Chevy Impala – LS402
4-Way Stop – LS403
Tail Light – LS404

2018

Myocardial Contusion – LS405

Lament
Bloodshot – LA501
Slit Wrist – LA502
Ruby Slippers – LA503
Venlafaxine Hydrochloride 150 mg – LA504
Nana's Patchwork Quilt – LA505

Lust + Lie
Stiletto – LU601
Pouty Lip (formerly Lipstick) – LU602
Satin Tie – LU603
Wife's Scream – LU604
Blocked Call – LU605

Leave + Land
Cat Eye Frames – LE701
Laser Removal – LE702
Sublet Kitchen – LE703
Subway Seat – LE704
Potted Geraniums – LE705

BUT IT IS DARK

JENNIFER FLISS

I am twenty-two feet above New York City. Below me, the glistening Hudson River, reflecting the lights of Manhattan and of New Jersey, across the way. In front of me is the gaping hole that used to be the Twin Towers. Tonight, two perpendicular blue lights shine into the clouds. Chalk coats my hands, ripped skin stings my palms. When the bar comes back to me at the platform, I will try the layout again. And again. And again. I have yet to catch it and what is trapeze if you're not catching your tricks? Lista! I call. The catcher shouts, Hep! I pull the bar up and toward me and I jump off the platform.

Sweep—I kick back my legs; years of gymnastics kept me limber. Force out—legs together, toes to the sky. Hollow—a deep round in my gut. Another sweep. Seven—eyes over the bar; see the lights of where the towers once stood. Set—hold, hold, hold, even as physics wants to peel my body off and drop it into the net below. And then, release and flip with my body as straight as I can. If I fly far enough, the blue lights will engulf me and carry me up.

* * *

One year later, my father dies. In my sleep, we sit together on a knoll. He is, surprisingly, alive again. Up here, the sun is larger. That's because it is setting for the last time. Somehow I know this, though I can't explain it. I tell my father to leave. We descend on opposite sides of the small hill. When the sun finally falls, later that day, I am alone in a shed in my backyard. That the sun will not rise again is not the apocalyptic event we were told it would be. I am safe, without the sun. Without the heat.

But it is dark.

It was always dark.

I am twelve and standing in the hallway of our apartment building, orange and brown speckled carpet, the smell of stale curry in the air. I notice the light by our door has gone out. Our apartment door, several inches of thick steel, is right across from the elevator. I push the button to call the elevator and I hear two dull thuds from inside our apartment. One. Two. I know my father is angry because one of the kittens peed on the couch. He comes out of the apartment, his great heft, breathing heavy, carrying a black trash bag, weight sagging in the middle. The bags are so shiny. We aren't allowed to have pets in the building anyway.

Years later, I have another dream. I am in a motel, one of those old-school fifties ones where the signs are neon and the hallways are outside and the folks who work there are always playing cards behind the counter. Pablo Picasso has been chasing me for a while. I am out of breath and almost out of options. Second floor. I judge how injured I'd get if I jumped. These rooms have kitchenettes. I grab a knife—a butter knife—from the drawer. The door opens. Picasso glares at me. You would think his features would be block-like and confused, nose where his ears should be, eyes where his heart should be. But he just looks like an artist. Intense, intelligent, criminal. He takes several steps toward me. I ready my butter knife. Then he turns, opens a closet, and steps inside.

* * *

I am a mother now. I stand in my kitchen, deriving great satisfaction from peeling vegetables. Not potatoes. Definitely not potatoes. But carrots, parsnips—the long ones. The zhush of the skin coming off in such delicate fine slices feels a little like pulling away a façade. I feel powerful. And then I feel naked.

In fantasies and in nightmares, I wear a red dress in a black and white world. I flit between trees and often just catch a glimpse of myself, a trail of red. It is like a drop of blood.

OTHER THINGS LOST

HANNAH GORDON

I was an athlete in junior high and high school. I used to go to practice four times a week: run drills, do circuits in the weight room, lose my breath to sprints. I would have said I was good; others might have, too. I was tall, and aggressive, which is a good combination in contact sports.

When I lose my reflexes, jumping becomes hard and suddenly everyone else on the court begins to look like someone who could send me to the hospital.

These are the side effects of vincristine, the first chemotherapy drug I'm on, thirteen-years-old: abdominal cramps, weight loss, nausea and vomiting, mouth sores, diarrhea, loss of appetite, taste changes, peripheral neuropathy.

Peripheral neuropathy is common. But it is serious. It includes decreased sensation and paresthesia (numbness and tingling) in the hands and feet. It can lead to loss of reflexes.

My oncologist taps my knees lightly with the end of her stethoscope. I wait for my legs to jump in response.

They hang there, limp. Dead.

This is normal, she tells me.

* * *

The cancer chews holes in my bones.

I lose pieces of my skull. Here, the surgeon scrapes the tumors out, replacing them with metal plates and screws that freeze during the winter, giving me blinding headaches.

I lose pieces of my vertebrae.

Pieces of my ribs.

A piece of my humerus.

A tiny piece of my shoulder.

A couple of pieces of my shin.

I ache all over. Each spot feels like a tender bruise. Some days, it feels like my bones may break altogether.

Cancer is hungry.

* * *

Since I'm tall, I always played the front row in volleyball. Sometimes center, where I blocked hits from the other team and called for the setter to send the ball my way.

After I start chemo, though, playing center becomes hard. Jumping becomes hard. My vertical suffers. It feels impossible to get off the ground.

For such a tall girl, you'd think she could jump higher.

I quit playing my junior year. I'm tired of trying to hold onto something I can't keep anymore. The team will be just fine without me.

I quit basketball, too. It becomes terrifying to steal the ball from the other team. Instinctually, I shrink away from it, worrying it might hit me in the head. Worrying it might split my stitches.

* * *

I lose a lot of weekends.

Side effects of Ara-C, the second chemotherapy drug I'm on, fifteen-years-old: headaches, low blood counts, dizziness, loss of appetite, eye pain, flu-like symptoms, neutropenia.

Neutropenia is an abnormally low level of neutrophils. Neutrophils are white blood cells that fight infection.

My first post-chemo fever strikes the night I'm camping with my friends at the county fair. I wake up shivering. Pull the sleeping bag tighter. It is July, and the air outside the trailer is sweltering. Inside, my teeth are chattering. I toss and turn all night, shaking so badly the sides of my stomach and my legs begin to ache from it.

I don't have my license yet: I cannot drive myself home. I don't wake up my friends' parents and ask them to take me home; I don't want them to feel sorry for me. Instead, I wait until 7 A.M. and text my older sister to pick me up ASAP. By then, my whole body is sore from shaking all night.

She sticks a thermometer under my tongue: I'm running a fever of 103. My parents are gone for the weekend, so she takes me to the hospital. I'm admitted to the E.R. later that day, and the doctors begin a course of antibiotics, hoping my neutrophil levels rise by the following morning. They assure me this is normal after a treatment.

This is the first of many weekends I spend like this, instead of hanging out with my friends. I miss countless sleepovers. I miss the best lake party of the summer.

My friends text and say they miss me. I turn my phone on silent. Listen to the beeping of the machines instead.

* * *

Peripheral neuropathy can lead to dropping in your feet.

It's already hard enough to walk down the hallway at school. Adolescence is a nightmare—you think everyone is always looking at you and laughing.

Sometimes, they are.

It takes a lot of focus to walk to classes without tripping over my own feet. Sometimes, I can go a whole day without doing it. Most of the time, not. I don't lift my feet high enough off the ground. The toe of my shoe catches on the carpet. I stumble, put my hands out to break my fall.

I become known as a klutz.

* * *

I lose a lot of blood.

Tube after tube of it. Some days, it is ruby red. Other days, dark as mud. It is thicker than I thought it'd be.

I'm studying biology in school, so one day I ask the nurse if the blood and plasma will separate, like oil and water, if left out long enough.

It's a question I'm proud to ask. Look at me. A good student asking questions about her body, about the things that get taken out of it.

I don't know. We don't leave it sitting out long enough.

* * *

Reflexes aren't always physical.

I miss more school than I want to. Most days, I force myself to go, despite the dull ache in my head. Despite the waves of nausea that pummel my stomach.

Despite having chemo in the morning. If we hurry, I can make it back in time for A.P. English.

I earn the nickname "School Skipper" anyway. I hear the popular boys shout it through the halls when they see me. Supposed friends. Everyone laughs when they do.

What's up, School Skipper?

Must be nice to be a School Skipper!

The girl I used to be—the girl who wasn't afraid to take a charge on the basketball court, who'd plant her feet firmly and let the other team run straight into her—would've have fought this nickname. She would have been fiery. She would have demanded it stop.

The girl I became, though, just lets it happen. Again and again. I have other things to fight.

* * *

I lose energy.

I lose time.

I lose bone density.

I lose muscle tone.

I lose.

I lose.

I lose.

And the cancer keeps winning.

* * *

The third type of chemotherapy drug I'm on, sixteen-years-old: a "maintenance" round. Light. Easy. Designed to kill any last cells that got left behind. This is supposed to be the easiest one of all.

Before—back when I was thirteen and first found out I was sick, when the doctors told me I needed chemotherapy—a teacher told me I was lying. He said I just wanted attention.

I still had my reflexes at this point. Physical, at least. I didn't react. At least not in front of him.

Later, I cried. And then I didn't cry again for a very long time.

* * *

The maintenance chemo lasts a year. At the age of seventeen, I am declared *in remission*. I lose a lot of things to cancer, but not my life. It will never take that from me.

Five years later, at my yearly checkup with my pediatric oncologist, my doctor taps my knees lightly with the end of her stethoscope.

My legs soar for the first time in ten years.

FOUR FLASH PIECES

OLIVIA DUNN

New Job

The Financial Adviser came for the "new employee" one-on-one. I imagined he was a robot with a cage under his shirt: his eye contact was too prolonged but not in a probing way, in a programmed way, and he spoke the word "emotional." I tried to ask broad questions about money as a conceptual force but his robot shoes were magnetized to the track.

At first, I tried to get a read on him but quickly became distracted by the idea of getting rich by giving three hundred of my barely-earned dollars to Philip Morris.

"Look at my shirt," I tried to say, with my eye contact. "It's from Goodwill."

I was a twenty-five-year-old secretary wearing expired lipstick and dirty white sneakers. There is a baby grand piano in my parents' house but besides that I expected to live in the backseat of an automobile for most of my 30's, like Paul Simon sang about.

Vetiver and Spice

I met a woman at a Berkeley gallery who smelled like pine trees and longing. Essence of vetiver, she told me. The smell Proust hates, I said. That was more or less the end of our conversation. I turned to look at one of the gallery walls, which at the time were covered in baskets made out of dried tubes of seaweed.

Vetiver is the smell that reminds the narrator of dragging himself to bed at night, ritual devastation to be separated from his beloved mother. Incense burning in his darkened bedroom, he hated to be wrenched from reality into sleep.

Last week the co-op was featuring a new organic deodorant for sale. Vetiver and Spice, it was called. I opened the bottle and breathed in. It smelled like pine trees and old wood floors and opening the oven to see if the pie is done. It cost nine dollars. I put it back on the shelf. I picked it up again. I put it back. I, too, am trying to be more in touch with reality. The reality of my bank account is in direct conflict with the reality of my desires, however, so I picked it up again.

Upon closer inspection, the label on the deodorant revealed that it is manufactured in Cambridge, NY. If I wrote a book about my own childhood, Cambridge would be my Combray, in a way. It is the former home of my eldest aunt, the location of our family Christmases, a wedding, a funeral. There is the wooden house where I tasted my first glass of wine, where I learned to use ammonia to clean the windows, where I rested from sunburn on the Oriental rug.

The sticker was a sign. I would be forced to purchase it. I could unify my whole personal history into my present identity with this significant co-op purchase. Vetiver and Spice and Olivia Dunn. My own body heat would become a machine of nostalgia. Perhaps I would even be stopped by another admiring woman, wondering about my striking scent.

Nine dollars plus tax and one blistering skin rash later, I'm back to my old unscented Liquid Rock roller ball. When I do write my memoirs, I will associate the smell of vetiver with the odd shape of seaweed baskets and the hot feeling of two sore armpits. And when I am older maybe I will get over the idea that buying things is any kind of real action towards the solidification of identity, that longing for something past or future is perhaps not any way to be in touch with reality.

Living Alone

Living alone means I am sitting here wondering how much longer until the early-early Midwest edition of the *Sunday Times* gets dropped off on the sidewalk in front of this apartment building. There is something unhealthy about craving the bright connection of a morning when it is only yet this late Saturday evening. It feels depraved, sneaking out into the damp night in one's pajamas, scooping up the baby-shaped delivery, running upstairs and relieving it, gently, of its bright blue bunting.

(Living alone means there will be no one to watch as I strip away each gray layer in a deliberate and guilty hunt for the Vows section.)

Living alone means I will read something fantastic just before bed and then I will dream about it. In the dream I will tell someone It's so real, this essay is so fucking real! When I wake up, I will remember saying it but not who to. Oh, it was no one. It could only be no one.

Though I don't sleep alone: every night, the stack of books at the foot of my bed grows higher. We crawl in together, gleeful, ambitious, and while the lights are on we can be comfortable lovers. When the room is dark and I am asleep at last, they grow jealous and head for the edges. I startle awake to the vengeful sound of their spines cracking as they hit the floor.

Oregon

The weather here was designed for the human body, even if these cut-off shorts were not. Sun alternates shade down the side street, providing alternating and equally pleasant cooling and warming air vectors. Trees and leaves drip down, resting, but not exhausted. Rust climbs happily along these old parked VWs, in no real hurry to decompose. Vines full of unnecessary flowers unfurl at their own damn leisure. The woman at the food co-op accepts my joke about no-coffee-not-awake-yet, as though it is a new and delightful concept. The men here look at me un-carnally, romantically, even, as if to wish I might soon cook them a healthful breakfast. Today and yesterday and tomorrow's weather will all be the kind of day you only get one or two of in New York, the scarcity of which drives me into a small hysteria of shoulds, a tight longing that cancels out the deep calm of a life-affirming 71 degrees Fahrenheit.

BLACK SNAKE

NANCY ALLEN

It was too tangled in landscape mesh to free itself,
flies already swarming its promising stillness.

I ran the half-mile home for scissors and back,
willing it to hang on, like a medic over the damaged

body of a child. While I cut the mesh, careful
not to nick its skin, the snake heaved up an entire

bird it did not have a chance to digest. The bird's
panicked cheeping and thrashing wings in the mesh

must have lured the snake in. Perfect body the size
of my thumb, its feather tips the color of sky.

Freed now, the snake curves off into weeds and I
wonder if I reached it in time. Is it too weak to live

or did I save it to prey again? Rescuers don't ask
I suppose—they can't tend to the child but leave

the driver who hit him to gasp his last in a ditch.

THE HOPEFULS

SUZANNE DOTTINO

The hopefuls are desperate to be seen. They wear identical black leotards that cling tightly to their prepubescent bodies. Their right hand rests lightly on the barre as they lift their legs above their heads and hold them there for a count of four. They stand in perfect uniformity, fully assimilated along the perimeters of a white room streaked with mirrors. A corpulent woman with apricot hair, thick stockings and wearing black orthopedic shoes that can't manage her bunions, taps her stick on the Marley floor. In a thick Russian accent shouts Pointe. Point. Pointe.

The hopefuls stare at their exquisite sweaty selves in the mirror as they point and flex, step on Rosin, stretch their arches, stand on their toes, arch their backs and bend backwards, fold themselves in half, wrap their feet around their heads, jump high in the air and land without making a sound, turn once, twice, three, four times, on one leg, plié, Grande plié, tendu, pas de bourrée, glissade, jete and walk like ducks, their bun heads held high and their spines, stick straight.

The hopefuls are rail thin and profoundly hungry. They carry bags on their bony shoulders the size of Carry-On luggage. Things they carry: 2 pairs of ballet slippers, 2 pairs of pointe shoes: one soft, one hard, 2 leotards, 2 pairs of tights, ankle, calf, arm and leg warmers, massage ball, foot roller, cosmetics bag, hairspray, first aid kit, "toe bag," lambswool, extra Band-Aids, KT tape, sewing kit, chocolate laxatives, antiperspirant, chocolate Ex-Lax, sugarless gum, cigarettes, Gummy Bears, Tic Tacs, caffeine drops, almonds, wallet, Marc Jacobs Body Mist, iPod, textbooks and a food diary

Hours before the hopefuls' class begins, they can be found in the hallways wrapped in cellophane-like pants and tops, layered and draped in colorful woolen one-piece body warmers, cut t-shirts, hand knit calf warmers, converted pajama tops, tailored sweat shirts and fuzzy foot warmers. They splay their dance bags and its contents, covering the entire width of the corridor with their bodies and their stuff, as they stretch, chew gum, zone out with ear buds in, wrap and re-wrap and an injury, brush their hair, sew their toes shoes, inspect their toes, inspect other's toes, roll a ball under their buttocks, and chat.

One hopeful stands on her right leg facing the wall as she slides her left leg up the wall so high and so close that her crotch touches, like a split on the floor, but vertical.

Athletes in team sports, performers in show business all believe that if you want it bad enough you'll make it. You'll win a game. You'll win a part. Luck could strike at any moment. You just have to wait it out and if you want it badly enough, you'll overcome all obstacles.

The hopefuls could want it until they are blue in the face, but if they are not born with certain physical attributes they can't have it. Ever.

Period.

Necessary physical attributes are: thin long-limbed bodies, a substantial amount of turnout (range of motion in the hips), beautifully arched feet, a small head. Musicality, élan, or that indescribable something such as raw talent that a hopeful might have, over one that doesn't, doesn't necessarily trump a hopeful endowed with the above physical attributes chances of making it. These attributes make beautiful lines and beautiful lines make beautiful shapes, and beautiful shapes inspire choreographers, who are among the key people, a hopeful wants to be seen by. If their bodies don't make beautiful lines, they won't be looked at. If they can't see you, (or won't' look at you; same thing) you won't be looked at. You might as well kill yourself.

Period.

Can a hopeful overcome the terrible tragedy that genetics have played on them? Hopefuls who are not born with a substantial amount of turn-out can gain some measure of it by lying face down on the floor, spreading their legs to a forty-five degree angle, bend at the knees so that the bottoms of their feet touch, have another hopeful sit on top of their feet, the weight of which will force the muscles around the hopeful on the floor's hips to release—or tear—usually the latter—but hopefully the former—so that their hips will open, and hooray, their feet will touch the ground, thus increasing their turnout. Until that day, they repeat this ritual—until that happy day arrives—and if it doesn't, they fake it. Faking it means turn her feet out, literally, making it appear as if her hips are open, completely disregarding the anatomical fact that her knees and hips are in opposition to what she is making her feet do.

The result is two-fold: the lines they make are more beautiful, on the other hand this near guarantees rheumatoid arthritis, knee and/ or hip surgery and replacements are their future.

Hopefuls who accept their turn-out-deprived bodies and who have innate (superior) technical skills, have a shot at being looked at seriously by teachers, choreographers, and most importantly, the audience. It happens. But what the audience really wants to see; what they are paying top dollar for is perfection not exceptions.

The hopefuls' skin is to be that of a color of a fresh peeled apple. Inside the dressing room as they change into their leotards, as they stand in front of the mirror and scrutinize every ounce of flesh on their lithe bodies, as they examine the small lip of butt cheek that they cover over with their leotard, as they apply eyeliner, lipstick and rouge, and during every moment of their one and a half hour class, the hopefuls are sizing each other up: This one's heads too big, this ones feet are sloppy, this one only eats condiments, this one can't jump, this one's father's on the board, this one hasn't had her period in six months. They compare toes. This one's second toe is bigger than her first: the pressure won't distribute equally; compared to my square toes, theirs are the most likely to injure first. This one in the advanced class had her breasts reduced, this one's torso is too long, this one barfed in the bathroom stall before class, this one's got it all but she's lazy, this one's hips are too wide, this one's neck is too short, this one's black.

In the dining hall of Jessica's Women's Residence, while Amber is on her way to the subway, as Pilar waits on line at Starbucks for her morning coffee, while they're stretching, or walking up and down stairs and all throughout their history, English, French, trig class, as they dream, even, the hopefuls are counting. 1, 2, 3, 4, 5, 6, 7, 8 ... 1, 2, 3, 4, 5, 6, 7, 8, and a one and a two ... and a 5, 6, 7, 8 ... 16 counts of four ... 4 counts of 8 ... 24 counts of 6, 0 percent fat, 2 ½ grams of fat, 16 oz., 24 oz. Apple: 85. Bagel: 260. Carrots 35. Muffin: 310, Yogurt: 120. Gum: 6 calories. The hopefuls' parents too are counting: Toes shoes: $80 (2 pairs per week). Tights: $20 Leotards: $40. Ballet paraphernalia: $50 here, $50 there. Winter, spring, summer and fall tuition

Stress levels spike when an outsider enters the hopefuls' classroom. The hopefuls jockey in line to be front and center. The hopefuls use peripheral vision to keep track of the number of corrections, glances, flirtations and proximity the guest teacher, choreographer, board member, trustee room gives to one hopeful and not another. The hopefuls assess: What's so great about her? My feet are prettier. I am exquisite. Look how sensitively I can portray my every movement. I am the fastest. Look at the openness across my chest, and the air underneath my chin. My jumps are higher, cleaner. My arches: gorgeous, my legs; longer and thinner, my turnout; natural. I have the most graceful arms, the prettiest fingers; my French Twist elongates my already long Swan Lake neck. How elegant my profile. Look how I can strikingly portray mystique, cheekiness and flirtatiousness through the use of my head/eyeline. Look how I engage my back muscles to make my arms more expressive. Keep your eyes on me. I am your muse.

Look at me.

Look at me.

Look at me.

Hopefuls think with their bodies.

How they "do" in morning class determines how they will know if they are up or down, good or bad, worthy or unworthy. Morning class is the spine of the hopefuls' day. If they have a bad class, and are "off their leg" or 'out of it' they can never get "it" back. The hopefuls wait in a state of heightened anticipation for their teacher to arrive, and for morning class to begin. Some sit and stretch, some stand, others primp and pluck at their bodies, buns, toe shoe ribbons, leotards, tights, as they look at the clock. When the teacher arrives, silence reserved for the only the holiest of places descends. The hopefuls line up at their place at the barre, stand in first position. The teacher demonstrates the plié combination, marking the movements with their hands, then nods to the pianist.

Winter, Spring, Summer, and Fall, six days a week, for years, adding up to decades, the hopefuls grow up together, in the classroom.

They watch their bodies change, they watch their classmates bodies change, they watch their teachers watching them, change, they watch the light in the classroom, depending on the season, change. They sensate the mood in the classroom; electric, somber, one day Amber is having a good day, one day Rita is on fire, one day Betsy is off.

Unlike the kind of "we're all in this together" kind of camaraderie that accrues from people spending that much time together, theirs is rife with competition. Their goal is not to be in it together, it is to be solo(ist).

There is no loneliness like theirs.

You, line up. You: go over there, you: stay put, you: stay in line, you; stop hiding in the corner, you; in front, you: POINTE, POINTE, POINTE, You: where are your feet? You, head up, look front, where are your arms? You're slow. You're late. Don't get ahead of the beat. Get those legs in the air. Front row: higher, higher, higher, faster, faster, and faster.

Yanking, kicking, beating, jumping, holding, squeezing, leaping, turning, bending, holding, pushing, smearing, lifting, day after day after day after day. Eventually, a hopeful will slip, fall, twist, buckle, over-stretch, tear, break or bruise, a bone, tendon or ligament.

The hopefuls pack up their photos of Gram and Grandpa, Junior, Spot, Mom and Dad, posters of Taylor Swift; pillows shaped like lips, Raggedy Anne dolls,

Glitter unicorns, fairy lights, bejeweled jewelry boxes, then seal the box up and it get shipped to student housing, a women's residence, a two-bedroom apartment with four other hopefuls, or with a friend of a friend who has a spare room in their apartment, on the Upper West Side of Manhattan. The loneliness of that first week away from home is unmitigated by Skype, text or phone. A more sensitive hopeful might react to the vast and varied opportunities of the city, so readily available, by losing their shit in a Bushwick bar, bingeing on Krispy Kreme, jars of cake frosting, or finding herself in an UBER on her way to LaGuardia for the next flight home.

Invitations the hopefuls get in the city and which they say yes to read like this: We request the honor of your presence (to decorate) a donors' cocktail party/fundraiser. After a few elbow ribbing from a more experienced hopeful, the newer hopefuls learn not to gawk or giggle when they enter buildings with doormen, housekeepers, chefs and musicians. The hopefuls wear strappy black dresses/and hold glasses of champagne while standing, feet turned out, on penthouse terraces overlooking the city. Men, older even than their father's, fawn over them, invite them out to restaurants, order them Peking duck and offer them smooth silent drives through Central Park in a warm limousine

A hopeful's dedication to their art is equal to their ability to hide pain. Bloodied toes, bruises, muscles pain, in time become so normal they don't feel it. Adrenaline, vanity and self-preservation kick in, their minds tell them to suck it up, hold it together, push harder and most importantly—smile.

Save it for when you retire.

Injured hopefuls, propped up by crutches, on the floor under the barre, or worse, wearing street clothes, is a sour reminder of what could happen to any one of them at any moment. The injured hopeful feels the pain of her injury far less than what she sees in the uninjured hopefuls gaze; you blew it. More for me. Go Away. Move on. You're blocking my view in the mirror.

Some hopefuls' parents' were once hopefuls themselves. They see their hopeful as 'a thing' that will fill their emptied life, fulfill the accomplishments and live the dreams that they, for whatever reasons, could not.

They are the ones brushing and pulling their hopefuls hair tight, tight, tight, sticking flowers into their hopefuls' elaborately constructed buns, French twists or crown of braids. They wait for their hopeful at the classroom door with an eye and a mouth full of criticism. The hopeful feels the way they are looked at and resent it. Ex hopefuls and hopefuls spend an extraordinary amount of time together. Their lives are inextricably bound by the production of ensuring a hopeful's success, in all the ways that the ex-hopeful failed. Sacrifices (real and imagined) an ex-hopeful makes for her hopeful: the best years of her life, her marriage, her having anything left to give to her other children, her figure, etc. The weight of these sacrifices feels real and lay heavily on the hopefuls' bony shoulders. They respond in not so pretty ways. One ex- hopeful gained so much weight she was asked to leave the school. One lost so much weight; her body started to growing moss on her skin keeps her organs warm. Another was chronically injured. Like trying to feed a hungry ghost, all hopefuls' attempts to satiate their ex-hopeful parent will fail, yet they'd risk dying trying.

Hopefuls in the corps de ballet of Swan Lake, say, must blend in neatly, yet she will want to have ownership of her work, to know it so well that it becomes a part of her, her movements conveying thoughtfulness, care and a mindfulness of classical purity, without ever becoming robotic. She will add her own subtle individual interpretation not only for herself but also for that person sitting in the fourth ring, looking at her through their binoculars. They will see her individual stamp and not a blur of identicals, wearing identical costumes, performing identical movements at precisely the same moment, performance after performance after performance, after performance.

When a working hopeful has reached complete mastery, she is now on her way down. The clock ticks louder than ever. The true grasping starts. When a hopeful has willingly or unwillingly stopped being a hopeful, she will struggle with adjusting to life without her umbilical barre.

When I am no longer a hopeful, who am I?

All hopefuls are of exceptional intelligence.

College, graduate school, medical school, they earn PhDs, become psychiatrists, interior designers, professors, museum scholars, choreographers, lighting designers, real estate magnates, scholars, philanthropists, they teach dance, they marry, they have children, their bodies fill out, they stay stick thin, they tend to their chronic hip, knee and foot injuries.

Hopefuls who cannot find an answer remain suspended, like an insect trapped in amber, in the past. They can be seen nibbling from salad bars, lingering in the corner of an 'open' advanced ballet class, their feet crooked with massive bunions, toes sticking up, draped in layers upon layers of loosely fitted, loosely stitched, torn, off-pink wool body warmers, a ravaged ballet skirt, untied toe shoes, ribbons flowing, sharp, short streaks of red rouge on their ashen cheeks, a pink tattered scarf attempting to hold their up their orange hair, in a messy bun.

When they look at themselves in the mirror, they see themselves as young, beautiful, turned out at the hip, able to remember complex combinations, backward and forwards, as being able balancing on one leg, triple pirouetting and leaping across the studio like a gazelle in the Serengeti.

When one ex-hopeful catches another ex-hopeful's eyes on the street, they silently acknowledge the shared past, but not each other, and keep walking.

DISTANCE

LAURA A. ZINK

So the plan was like this—we'd tell him we could score some weed, we'd take him into an alley, and then, we'd mug him. It was a rotten idea. Kind of a bullshit thing to do on my part, too. But so much garbage was coming at me that day. Real rapid fire. Like there was the money, of course. Fashion, I guess. Robitussin. Nirvana. Some dude crapping himself. A girl. I don't know. Hella shit. It just sort of happened.

The day started off pretty normal. I woke up under the bridge with the Newell Punx around noon and went to Creek Liquors to spend the last of my GA check on a bag of Top tobacco and a bottle of Mad Dog 20/20 Grape. Around four or five, we went to the park and sat around on the grass, rolling cigarettes, drinking, and talking about maybe shoplifting something to trade for meth later on. Typical Monday.

It didn't get weird until Janie sat next to me. God, you should have seen her: big tits, pink Bettie Paige haircut, deep green eyes, nice legs. She looked way older than fifteen. She wasn't the kind of girl who'd look twice at a dude like me either, mainly because she could go back to her folks' house whenever she wanted. But there were a bunch of those house-punk types around. Like Nirvana got famous, and all these rich kids wanted to play orphan. Most of them were assholes hogging up the spare change, but not Janie. She wore rich kid real different. At least, to me. You might think I'm weird, but I thought of it this way—if she let me get with her, she'd be saying what I had was better than nice parents and a soft bed and money. Being twenty-one and legit homeless pushing five years, screwing Janie would've been a real big ego boost. I had to go for it.

So we were sitting in the park, and I noticed it was pretty overcast. I thought it was a good enough time to move in on her, so I handed her my army jacket. She scrunched up her nose and waved me off. That made me feel like a jerk, so when she grabbed the bottle of Mad Dog out of my hand, I didn't protest. I watched her drain it, too. She handed me the empty bottle and looked out across the park. Then, she whispered, "Oh my God. Dan, look."

I looked, but all I saw was a runty, blonde kid with his hands in his pockets, kicking at the dirt. He wore baggy jeans and an even baggier t-shirt that had this big cross with a red no symbol over it. I figured it was some kind of statement, but he couldn't have been older than twelve, so what the fuck did he know about anything? I pointed at him.

"That little kid?" I said.

"Shhh," she said. She grabbed my arm and pulled it down. Then, she put her mouth to my ear and with a breathy whisper, she's like, "He's a mark. Look at that wallet chain. One yank and we got his wallet."

At first, I thought she was kidding. Sure, the chain was ridiculous. It ran from somewhere under his t-shirt to his knee and back up in a silvery loop. And sure, it was dumb to advertise a wallet like that, but he looked like one of those foo foo "grunge" kids, and they all wore those stupid chains. We had plenty of crooks and junkies around town, too, but we weren't supposed to have muggings and SROs and tragic deaths and end-of-the-line shit like that. That was San Francisco stuff. Shit you had to take BART to get to. Janie didn't let up though.

"C'mon," she said. "We could get an eight ball and a room."

I had a sweet tooth for dope for sure, but my mind closed in on two words—*a room*. The other times any of us Newell guys had tried anything with her, it was under the bridge, so she'd say there were too many people around. So I thought, if I hooked up dope and a room, she'd sort of have to give in, right? And she had to know what she was asking me to do was a big deal. I had broken into houses and cars, but that was victimless stuff, or at least victimless in the sense that the "victim" was far away when it happened. No one was traumatized. Mugging was different. It's one of those stare-the-victim-in-the-face sort of crimes, something only legit bad guys did. And I didn't want to be that kind of guy, you know? And the kid was so young.

But then, I looked down at Janie, big green eyes peeking over my shoulder and hands tugging at my arm, and I just felt so lonely all of a sudden. What could I do? I said ok.

* * *

I walked over to the kid, smiling and holding out my bag of Top. I asked him if he wanted a smoke. In a voice way too deep to be natural, he said, "Yeah, bro. Dyin' for one."

He stuck his hand in the bag and pulled out a fat pinch of loose tobacco. He looked at it, put it back, stuck his other hand in the bag, and started fingering around. Clearly, the kid had no idea what he was doing, but I didn't want him to feel like a jerk. I pulled the bag back and told him I'd roll him one. While I was working on his cigarette, I tried to think of a way to start up some friendly chitchat. He was obviously the kind of kid who went to school, so I asked him about it. He got a real serious look on his face and stared out into the distance.

"Nah," he said. "I ditched that shit. Needed a day to chill out. Get my thoughts together."

I coughed to hide a laugh. "Yeah," I said. "It's tough out there."

Just as I handed him the cigarette, the sun started shining. My clothes started to roast and give off a sour, salty smell. It made me think about Janie turning up her nose at my jacket. My mom had a thing with smell. Used to say it was a bum's ID card, usually in reference to my dad. She told me I smelled like a bum once, right before she changed the locks on me for being strung out all the time. Thinking about that made me feel kind of embarrassed, so I crossed my arms and tried to cover it, hoping the kid wouldn't notice.

"So," I said. "Your mom know you're out here?"

"Nah, bro," he said. "She's hella square."

"Guess she doesn't like that shirt much either," I said and jerked an elbow at the slashed over cross.

He sniffed the air. "Fuuuck, bro," he said. He wiped the back of his hand against his nose and took a step back. And then, he's like, "God is for fucking feebs."

My first thought was, "Shit, I don't need a lecture from some dumbass kid." But then, I was so fucking glad he didn't say anything about the smell. And it wasn't like I could get a word in edgewise anyway. I mean, you wouldn't believe how much this kid talked. He told me about his step-dad being a dick and about his teachers being on his back and how his shirt was for Bad Religion, which was his favorite band, and he respected them even though they "sold out," but he was going to do them one better by starting a band and nev–er ev–er signing on a major label and getting owned by "corporate fuckwads and shit clowns." Honestly, I got a little kick out of it. I even started to remember how I felt that shit when I was his age. You know, "fuck authority" and ideals and dreams and crap. I hadn't gotten in a conversation like that for a long time. It felt kind of nice.

Then, Janie came over. "You want to buy some grass?" she said.

I was crazy pissed she did that. She had no appreciation for the trust and good social woo woo I was building with this kid. I nudged her on the shoulder, giving her that calm-the-fuck-down look. She pinched my side and gave me that what-the-hell's-your-problem look. Then, we both looked at the kid, stupidly, big smiles on our faces.

The kid wasn't paying attention. He stood there, lock of hair hanging over one eye, the other eye zeroing in on Janie's tits. The little perv had the same thing on his mind as I did. I clapped him on the shoulder and asked him his name. All he said was, "Huh?"

"Your name, kiddo," I said. "What is it?"

"It's Tyler," he said. He flipped his hair away from his eye.

"I'm Jon," I lied. "And this is Nicole." I pointed to Janie.

Janie crossed her arms over her chest and sighed. "You smoke weed, Tyler?" she said.

He flicked out his chin. "Hell yeah," he said. "I been tokin' for like … a year now."

It was obvious the little guy was lying, but Janie didn't seem to care. She kept at him, going on about how we could hook him up if he came downtown with us. I'm not sure if Tyler was excited about the drugs or the attention, but he had a light in his eyes and this big-ass, giddy smile on his face. Then, he's like, "Fuck yeah! That rules!" His voice totally cracked when he said it, too.

Janie snorted, grabbing her mouth and choking out these hard, nasally giggles. Tyler must have felt pretty dumb because he started walking out of the park ahead of us, shoulders slouching in some phony gangster act, wallet chain sparkling one last time before the sun hid back behind the clouds. I grabbed Janie's hand and jogged us forward, but I was pretty pissed at how pushy she was being. She wouldn't give me the chance to figure out if the whole thing was a good idea or not, which I tell you right now, it wasn't.

* * *

I needed to buy myself some time so I could find a good alley to do this in. I told Tyler we needed to go to a special payphone to make sure the dealer would answer.

"The dude is crazy paranoid," I said. I tapped Tyler's shoulder with a friendly partner-in-crime kind of move. He looked at me and smiled a little, so I knew I was helping him forget how much Janie embarrassed him. And it seemed like he trusted me, too.

It was about that time I noticed Janie wasn't with us. I looked back, and she was trailing behind us, smoking a cigarette with one hand and twirling her hair with the other. She didn't have a care in the world. We had a plan to meet up at an abandoned house on Lily Street if we got separated, but I didn't think she was planning on us getting separated. So now I'm thinking, if I had to do everything by myself, I'd have to deal with the consequences by myself, too. And, if I didn't pull it off, Janie would never fuck me. And she'd probably tell the Newell Punx I was too chickenshit to take down a twelve-year-old, and then, they'd never stop shoving me around and stealing my shit. Like ever.

I shook it off and tried to keep the conversation going. I focused on the deal, talking about the size of the buds, saying they were as big as an eighth and all green and covered with purple crystals.

"Totally worth the price," I said. "Forty bucks an eighth is a steal."

Tyler nodded and said, "Sure is, bro."

Since he seemed cozy with forty bucks, I decided to push it a little further.

"You could get a half for a hundred probably," I said. I eyeballed him. The price didn't faze him at all. I pressed on, making him another cigarette, scanning the side streets, and continuing on about the buds. He looked at the ground as I talked, nodding along with whatever I said. But after a few blocks, I ran out of stuff to say.

Before there was even three seconds of quiet, Tyler's like, "My pops used to drink Robitussin. Like 'til he was whacked out and trippin', bro."

That shook me. I didn't say it, but I'm thinking, "Seriously? You want to talk dads?" I mean, who does that? You didn't see me whining to him about my dad. Like I'm going to be all, "Yeah, my pops drank himself to death in an SRO in SF." No fucking way, right? Because it wasn't shit for regular conversations, especially with strangers. I tried to ignore it, but he kept going. Evidently, his pops was in some kind of hospital.

"He's wet-brained now," he said. "He shakes and shits his pants."

And what the fuck was I supposed to say to that? There I was, trying to figure out a side street or an alley to mug this kid, and he's getting crazy personal with me. I got a vision of Tyler standing over his wet-brained father at the hospital, looking down at his drooling face and shaky hands, missing him and feeling betrayed at the same time. I started thinking about how he was probably made fun of at school for having an alcoholic dad who shits his pants. Poor kid probably got all red-faced, balling his fists and holding back tears, fucking laughter echoing in his ears. People made fun of my dad, too, but what did the kid think I was, a therapist?

I looked behind me, and Janie was closer than before, only a half block away. I flicked my head once to call her over. She flipped me off. I opened my eyes real wide and clenched my jaw, trying to drive home how urgent it was she come and help me. She looked away and waved me forward like I was a little kid. Completely shut me out.

And Tyler kept talking. I tried to look interested and thoughtful, wrinkling my brow and cupping my chin, but I didn't want to hear it anymore. The craziest thing was, the longer I tried to block out his voice, the more I saw him. His hands were little and clumsy. His skinny fingers held his cigarette like a joint. He didn't even inhale it right, just sucked in a cloud and blew it right back out. He was trying so hard to act cool and grown. And the more I looked at him, the more I felt like a twelve-year-old kid again. I could almost see myself standing at the edge of the park, wearing a Testament t-shirt and that stupid latchkey tied around my neck with green yarn, wishing someone would think I was cool so I didn't have to go back to my mom's crappy, empty apartment and be bored by myself the rest of the night.

While I was going through all this, the sun came out again. Everything around me got painful and shiny, even Tyler. His shirt, too. It went hard crazy white, that stupid red no symbol bleeding through, the fucking cross. It made me think about fate, that maybe what was happening was bigger than screwing Janie. Like maybe God wasn't just some feeb-magnet nobody, and Tyler met me for a reason. My first day at the park, all I got was metalheads buying me forties and laughing at me when I puked on myself. It was humiliating, but it wasn't enough to keep me from coming back and screwing up my life so bad that by the time I was grown, I was basically trying to mug my younger self. I looked at Tyler again, his stupid little skater haircut, his freckled kiddy face, the jerky nightgown-sized shirt, and I started to think if I scared him real bad, maybe I could change his path and make him turn out less like … well, less like me. You might think I'm crazy, but at that moment, I seriously thought mugging him was the nicest thing I could do.

So then ahead of me, about thirty feet away, I saw a small alley on the left. Where the sidewalk met the alley, there was a six-foot-tall chain-link fence. Ivy coated it from top to bottom, so whatever happened behind the fence was blocked from the street. Directly across the street from that, there was another alley, blocks long and covered on either side by three-story buildings. And behind me, just a few paces away, Janie started to hum real sweet and playful. On my left, Tyler jumped over puddles, skipping almost, smiling and clueless, puffing out little clouds of smoke. In front of me, the ivy-covered fence got closer and closer. It felt like a sign.

I grabbed his skinny shoulders and slammed his face into the fence. I got behind him and pushed him up against it, clutched his wallet chain, yanked, and ran across the street with the wallet in my hand. Once I got to the alley, I heard a loud voice behind me, high-pitched and urgent, "Run, Dan! Run!"

It was Janie. She screamed my real name, outing me to everyone in earshot. I charged forward, her voice getting fainter the farther I ran.

Once it disappeared, another voice rose up in its place, louder and higher-pitched than the first, "Fuck you, Dan! Give me my wallet!"

The little shit was chasing me. I heard his sneakers padding against the ground behind me. He was gaining on me fast. I changed course and ran to Main Street, hoping to lose him. I wove through the shoppers and darted into the street, running right down the middle until I saw an out-door tunnel on the left. I turned and took it. My boots smacked against the concrete. My breath echoed off the walls. Once I was halfway through, I realized all the sounds in the tunnel came from me. I had lost him.

I bent over and grabbed my knees, trying to catch my breath. I felt like I was going to puke, but I lifted myself up anyway and opened the wallet. There were a bunch of bills: a couple of tens, some fives and ones, a few twenties. It was enough to get dope, a room, and a little private attention from a green-eyed girl with a bad attitude. I could almost feel her tits in my hands.

As I'm counting the money, a scuffing, squeaking sound came from the other end of the tunnel, soft and faint at first, but it got louder. I turned and saw Tyler coming at me again, face red, arms pumping.

"My bus pass!" he screamed. "Just give me my bus pass!"

What was I supposed to do? Wait for him so I could return his bus pass? Stomach acid rising in my throat, I turned and ran again. Across the street, I saw another chain-link fence. There were thick hedges about three feet up on either side, and the fence itself was another three feet beyond that. I knew I'd have to leap over the bushes to reach the top of the fence, and if I could pull that off, I'd have to toss myself over the top far enough to avoid getting tangled in the three feet of bushes waiting for me on the other side. It was dangerous, but I had no other choice. I had to ditch this kid.

I booked across the street, gathering as much momentum as I could. Once the bushes were a few feet away, I leapt. I caught the fence with my hands and twisted my fingers through the chain links, straining to pull myself up. Boots scraping against the fence, I jerked up and heaved myself over. It was a blind drop, but I landed. Both feet on the asphalt, too.

In front of me, there was a small alley parking lot, and at the end of it, a thin passageway between two buildings. All I had to do was get through that, and it'd be a straight shot down State Street to the abandoned house on Lily where Janie was waiting inside.

As I ran to the edge of the parking lot, I heard a dragging sound— ping, ping, scrape, ping. There was a rustle of branches, and a hard thump, like a sack of meat hitting the concrete—thunk. Then, it was quiet, so quiet the air had a sound, almost like an echo. I turned, and the parking lot was empty. No Tyler anywhere. I should have been relieved, but all the quiet and emptiness was eerie. Something wasn't right.

I walked back to the fence. As I got closer, I heard whimpering in the bush. I looked over it. Tyler was flat on his back, right leg bent forward and twisted, bloodstain spreading across his jeans at the shin. My chest froze.

"Why the hell did you run after me?" I said. I stared at him, waiting for an answer. He only winced. His eyes squeezed tight. His chin quivered. I wanted to put my hand on his shoulder, to comfort him or something, but when I reached out, my hand trembled. I pulled it back, held it to my chest.

"Can you hear me, kid?" I said.

He nodded and coughed out a few hard sobs.

"This was an accident," I said. "You can't blame me for an accident."

He shook his head, his eyes locking on some distant place in the sky. I looked, too. The only thing up there was a blanket of dark grey clouds. They rolled slowly over us. Just carrying on. Like nothing. We were alone. Two stupid, fucked-up kids in a dirty back alley. I looked down at the wallet. I knew what I had to do.

"I'll find a phone and call 911," I said. "I'll get you an ambulance, okay?"

Tyler wailed and burst into loud, gasping tears. "I want my mom," he said.

Everything around me dissolved: the buildings, the alley, the parking lot. I felt a spark of anger. He had his mom. And he expected her. He hurt himself chasing down some fucking criminal, and he expected her to make it better. And she probably would. She'd probably cry, too. Probably come to the hospital with that asshole stepdad who'd probably apologize for being a dick. Tyler would get better, and Tyler would start that stupid band that was like Bad Religion, and Tyler would finish high school and college and have ideals and dreams and live a long and wonderful life. And the biggest bitch, the biggest "fuck you" of them all was he wouldn't get anything unless I saved him first. And what could I expect for that? Time in jail? A bridge to sleep under? Some dumb girl who'd only fuck me if I had drugs or money? I'd been a kid standing at the edge of a park once, too, but no one came to save me. No one even spared a thought for me. For what happened to me. What would happen …

I pulled the money out of the wallet and stuffed it in my pocket. He owed me that at least. There was no way I could stay in town, so I left the bus pass in the billfold.

I leaned over Tyler and said, "Listen, kid. You don't know me. You never saw me. I don't fucking exist. And if you tell your parents or the cops I do, I'll find you and kill you myself." I dropped the wallet next to his head, chain and all. Then, I ran as fast as I could to catch the BART train out of town.

Once inside, I sat by the window. I could see the bridge, the park, and the abandoned house on Lily Street. Down State Street, the red lights of the ambulance flashed. I called that ambulance. It was the last thing I saw before the train hit the tunnel. I sat back and closed my eyes, turning my thoughts to the city. I saw a flash of Tyler's broken leg, his wincing face. My guts twisted and forced my eyes back open.

Two dark, cloudy eyes stared back at me. It was an old woman. Pink rain bonnet. Tan trench coat. She started and broke her gaze. I figured she was embarrassed, what with me catching her staring and all. And then, she lifted her purse. Wrapped her arms around it, too. Clutched it to her chest. I scanned the car. I needed one person, just one to acknowledge that the woman was crazy, that I wasn't the kind of guy who'd do something like that to an old lady. But everywhere I looked, bodies stiffened, purses and backpacks inched away, one gaze after another escaped mine in search of windows, watches, and floors. I felt so enormous and invisible at the same time. That feeling, it takes you to some way back place you didn't know you remembered. There's sun on the blacktop. The smell of tanbark. Jump ropes and swings. All the kids are laughing and huddling together. They're watching you without looking, whispering into their hands.

EXCERPTS AND ADDITIONS TO A PLANTATION OWNER'S DIARY

AILEEN BASSIS

I. February 1709

*I rose at 5 o'clock this morning and read a chapter in Hebrew
and 200 verses in Homer's Odyssey.*

He ate battered eggs and pork,
beef hash and buttered bread,

drank French wine and apple cider,
played dice and cards and walked about his land

but didn't give a name to the negro woman
who ran away three times:

One time, she left her hoe lying in a field.
One time she ran with a bit fixed between her lips.

He put her in a shack, tied her hands and feet.
She escaped when it was dark.

Some said she was free up north in Canada.
Others said she wandered, dying in the swamp-lands

among cypress trees and button willows
and vines of bittersweet.

II. October 1711

About 4 we dined. My man's horse was lame.
A stop along a journey,
a traveler's inn,
a narrow room lit
by a tallow candle—fleshy scent,
Footsteps above, below,
a whinny from the stable,
—door creaks.

At night I asked a negro girl to kiss me.
Soft He calls—grabs Her hand,
grass-stuffed mattress rustles, ropes sag.
Her eyes flicker a yellowing light.
Down She bends to press her plum lips
to bristles—tasting wine, tasting meat.

A vein along Her neck tightens
like a rein threaded through a ring
and She swallows as if Her mouth
held a stone digging along Her tongue.

Their shadow stretches up
the patterned wall, a shape
monstrous as a minotaur
with a great and nodding head
and blind-eyed tiny flowers flicker
in the candle's flame: some blue
some red, some pinker than a tongue
that darts between His teeth.

III. May 1712

My wife caused several of the people whipped
for their laziness ... I ate some boiled beef.

Cat-o-nine Tails:
      Nine Knotted Leather Lashes
     Oak Handle,
       Oiled
         Smooth

THE HILL

LAURA HUEY CHAMBERLAIN

The last thing she expects to see, the last thing she wants to see, is this line of boys running toward her on the trail, yipping like wolf pups, their chests bare even in the icy rain, running so easily while she has to fight for every goddamn breath to make it uphill, which should count as a staircase, really, because this hill's got a climb like nobody's business, but thank god she squelched her urge to walk, suffocated that whining bitch back before she heard the boys, back before she saw them, because what would it matter, really, if she walked the hill, with no one around to see, and with eight miles behind her it's not like she'd be wimping out, not like she wouldn't get all her steps in for the day, but nooo, she can't walk, not even one little step but who's she trying to fool, she's no athlete, everyone can see she might as well be walking, might as well be crawling, she's going so slow, and let's face it, even in her best years, even before she starting spitting out babies and her babies grew up and she got fat and old, even then she was never a runner, so now here she is, running up this hill in an ugly raincoat toward a line of yipping boys who are just now cresting the peak, swooping down on her, so young and so full of themselves, the whole goddamn lot of them, and all she can do is keep moving up the hill, stare straight ahead, try hard not to look at them, so hard that she almost misses her cue when the first boy stretches out his hand in a high-five, and then the second, and then the third, and then the whole long line of them.

VARIOUS HISTORIES OF SEA SERPENTS

ANITA GOVEAS

No one talks about what Nana keeps in the basement. You get used to the hollow thumping in the mornings, how she removes one worn chappal and bangs on the kitchen wall. You learn to put your whole focus, your whole being into the food you make together. Her appas are perfect, densely textured on the outside, hiding their sweetly slippery coconut centre.

Wriggling on your hard, narrow bed, sometimes you dream of twisting around frantically until you can hold your tail in your mouth. Rough ropes bind you because of your destructiveness, but you will cause your own ending. This is comforting, when the silence in the house makes you want to shed your skin. You scratch less at the pulse that jumps in your elbow, and the burning line between your budding breasts.

In history you learn of Ragnarok, the end of days. The walls of the classroom are full of tall, blonde heroes astride flaming boats and monstrous horses. Your drawing of Jormungandr, a black-haired, brown-eyed sinuous beauty who grows too big for the earth, lies in a drawer.

No one talks about why Nana has a basement. Apartment buildings flourish like palm fronds in Mumbai, fringed by corrugated iron shacks that people pass over. She looked out over toiling fishermen and angled trees, in broiling sun and roiling rain. In Kent, gardens are the treasure, the excuse to feel watery sun on parched skin. Your tired father and your ceaseless mother looked for eight months to find a house that Nana tolerated. One of her suitcases, tied up with blue string, was dripping. She never goes outside.

You fall asleep on the bus to sixth-form college, and imagine shattering earthquakes and virulent winds. Sometimes, at home, you awake from your internal vortex to a tremoring floor that stretches you out and relieves internal pressures. The bed vibrates, the walls shake, the oval box on top of the cupboard where you keep your secrets rocks from side-to-side. At the edge of sound, there are chipping noises, tiny hammers or a persistent chappal.

You read a book about the Bakunawa, the dragons who cause earthquakes and eclipses. You loop yourself in bedsheets and stare down the moon. It can only ignore you, and you're used to that. You draw craters and shadows, dark streaks of volcanic crust. Nana helps you make the roundest idlis from pounded rice, they shine like pearls. You suck them down slowly as if you can swallow all your problems.

No one talks about why Nana needs her basement, or why you need Nana. The days you wrap up in blankets and can't get out of bed, the squeezing headaches, the time your mother had to leave the office as you'd wedged yourself under a sink in the girl's toilets. The itch, itch, itch along your spine as if your skin will fissure.

You have visions of tangled limbs in the bath, as warm liquid saturates you, holds you down along your fault-lines. You're wrapped around the precious core of yourself, revealing this would bring untold disasters. There is a trial approaching, you can't hide from it but you can prepare.

You find a picture of a Naga, the serpent race, in your Nana's handbag. It's speckled with droplets, forgotten raindrops or ancient tears. You remember, from a time before, that treasure can be protected with weapons like venomous knowledge and fierce belief in unbreakable connections. You draw Nana making sweet crescent-shaped almond cookies. You smile with your eyes as you draw in their tails.

TWO RAPTURES

MICHAEL DIEBERT

1

If I stepped out of my body I would break*
into a dead run, and I do, barefoot,

suddenly and strangely naked,
down the deck steps, over the jutting rocks

and almost total absence of grass—
it's a yard for dogs—and there she is,

latte streak against the still-sleeping weeds,
sniffing around the fence-edge,

considering the bricks, tilting her head at me
quizzically—

my arms shorten to forelegs,
hands become paws, nose

a formidable and sensitive snout,
and just above where my butt once cleaved

2018

now sprouts a rascally tail
wagging furious loop-de-loops,

she and I bound by the same boundless code,
digging up the bones of bygone years,

barking in harmony at the garbage truck,
leaping at all small moving things.

First line taken from James Tate's poem, "A Blessing"

2

For I will consider my three-legged dog Berkeley.
For she has lived a long, full, cheese-block-eating, coffee-slurping, floor-licking life.
For she has barged through to sixteen, and barges on.
For she is a great conductor of deep feeling.
For she was once four-legged but cancer bloomed.
For she can pant.
For she drinks much water and would drink, I declare, the breadth and depth of the Chattahoochee.
For she has the softest head.
For I scratch behind her ears and believe for a moment I have it all figured out.
For I find solace in her white muzzle.
For it is the muzzle of the holy spirit.
For I know deep down she is a saint, and seeks the same.
For I have made for her a mighty resumé.
For she has skills: doctor, chef, advice columnist, meteorologist.
For no one can say she is not in constant pursuit.
For she tears into her senior formula food with the gusto of a puppy.
For I need not set an alarm.
For there is a thump like thunder from under the bed, and I pull her out and make it possible for her to stand.

For she is the dog I have always wanted to be.

For love is entwined with impatience and anxiety.

For when she is pacing and unsettled, I would give my leg for her to tell me what she wants.

For we give her much for what we presume is pain.

For she tests the stairs before she commits; here she is, hopping up, and I swear she is smiling.

For she wants only to be near.

For after all she has every right to smile.

For she follows me into the study, where the cushy bed awaits.

For this is a house of counsel and consolation.

For over the backyard I stand guard as she scouts out the best place to conduct her business.

For I clean her up when she leaks.

For I shall fill her water bowl until the river runs dry.

After Christopher Smart's "Jubilate Agno."

2019

GADO GADO

CLAIRE POLDERS

After my mother's funeral, I bike to The Hague's largest street market and fill myself with life—motions, scents, colors, sounds. I also make a pit stop in the neighborhood toko, a shop I've never set foot in before. Plump bags swing from my handlebars as I'm pedaling back to my childhood home.

I dump the groceries on the kitchen counter before opening the terrace doors. The house smells of death and the not-so-long struggle against it. Flowers of solace hang rotten in a vase. I haven't taken the time yet to throw them out or carry my luggage upstairs. With a thousand tasks crowding my list, I'm lost for a place to start, and therefore veer toward something that needs doing for reasons other than practicality.

I tuck a bottle of gewürztraminer in the fridge and lower a cookbook from the shelf.

Of course I went to her funeral—could I not have gone? My father was excused because of the oceans and continents that have been separating them for twenty years. I only had to take the train down from Haarlem, a thirty-minute ride. The sky was like marble this morning, frozen with swirls of clouds. I unpack my groceries in the relief that she is buried and I can move around unseen.

Out comes a sack of bean sprouts, two small Chinese cabbages, a fistful of red chilies, bagged shelled peanuts, a chunk of funky looking tofu, a carton of eggs, canned coconut milk, several wedges of copper-colored paste wrapped in cellophane, a container of fried onions, a bundle of green beans, transparent sachets of fluorescent spices called ketumbar and djintan, a root that may be ginger but isn't, bags of krupuk, a garlic bulb, a cauliflower, a cucumber, and one kilo box of long-grain rice.

The kind lady in the toko was patient enough to help me locate the ingredients she knew I would need. She threw in a slice of cinnamon spekkoek as a gift. My eyes must have been more swollen than I realized.

I thumb through the cookbook, virtually unused, glancing at pictures and names—Nasi Goreng, Babi Guling, Tongseng, Saté Ayam, Lumpia Semarang. Indonesia has more than thirteen thousand islands and as many recipes. With a steel ladle, I keep the book open on the page that tells me how to make Gado Gado (Mix Mix).

The last time I saw my mother, she looked like the bouquet of flowers I now find myself tossing in the compost bin outside. Her pale skin had begun to fold over its own wrinkles. I listen to the buzz of city traffic and the dialogues of birds. Back inside, the house surrounds me like an army base, devitalized by peace.

I haul out the colanders and bowls, select whisks and measuring spoons.

Unlike most mothers who lived to nourish their kids (it seemed), my mother never enjoyed feeding me. Cooking, like eating, was a necessity, a job that didn't call for elaborate hours behind hot skillets. I grew up on instant oatmeal, canned split-pea soup, and frozen pizzas burnt to a crisp. For my mother, taste was beyond the point. Probably because her appetite was equally beyond the point.

I scrub the cauliflower under running water. Rinse the sprouts and beans. Let them drain. Cut the cauliflower in bite-sized chunks and shred the cabbage. The slaughter of the raw.

It's a lie that you can't perform on drugs. A few white lines made my mother a high-functioning pro, focused, competent, working twelve hours a day. She was even sporty and health-conscious if you can believe it—sugar was way worse than coke. It was only when she came back from rehab that she acted sloppy and insecure, more critical of herself than of others.

I boil water, throw in the rice, time the eggs, and blanch the vegetables. After the eggs are hard-boiled, they will need to be peeled and quartered.

Her habit's occasional excessiveness made it a problem, though. She would talk superabundantly, from the moment she woke till the hour she slipped into unconsciousness. Strangely, she rarely spoke of reality. Her words conveyed how she thought the world ought to be: coffee hotter, cars faster, vodka cheaper, daughter more invisible.

I grill the peanuts in a casserole. Pulverize them in the food processor. Splash in the coconut milk. I suppress the urge to sample a bite. The brown sludge curls in the pan.

When my mother was high beyond the task she'd set for herself, she would latch onto other tasks, like cataloguing my outfits, postures, or facial expressions. Each time she lost control, a fury that had nothing to do with the situation was unleashed. People who witnessed this fury spoke of it with awe, as though it were an accomplishment. Perhaps it was; the rage got things done. She once punched the hotel manager who refused to take the Dionysus room off her bill after the overhead projector had stopped working halfway through her presentation. Although banned from the premises forever, she got her reduction.

I sauté chopped garlic and slices of Laos root. Measure out teaspoons of sugar.

My mother, a career coach, had one idol in life, Dr. Aletta Jacobs. In 1878, Aletta Jacobs was the first female student to graduate from a Dutch university. She also became the first female doctor in Dutch history. She advocated the use of a pessary for contraception, fought for women's suffrage, organized rallies, established societies, drew up petitions, and worked for world peace.

I wash and wafer the cucumber, salt it, and let it sweat. Bare naked. Then I fry the tempeh in palm oil until crispy.

Six-months pregnant, my mother dreamed of calling her unborn baby Aletta. My father, who didn't want to burden me with unattainable feminist expectations, proposed the laid-back name Laura. By way of response, my mother got high and challenged him to a game of Scrabble. She won, and I take the way this conflict played out as representative of the distribution of power in my parents' marriage. They divorced when I was nine.

I free the shrimp paste from its cellophane jail. Get the smelly gunk all under my fingernails.

There have been times that I was convinced my mother had grown to love me, her clever daughter who kept her nose clean. And I believed I'd grown to love her too, even though, or perhaps because, we rarely spoke to each other.

The beans feel fibrous on my tongue, the sprouts soggy. I taste and drain the rice—al dente. An odyssey of textures.

On the last day of our living together, a week before I would travel to Bali where I would spend the summer and more with my father's relatives, my mother prepared an Indonesian dish for me: Gado Gado. She hadn't told me about her plan in advance; it was either meant as a surprise or she'd cooked it up on impulse. I remember coming home in the late afternoon and being drawn into the kitchen by delicious smells. There she was, my mother, hair messy, hands greasy, an apron around her waist—what a sight! Noticing me, she grew excited, like a puppy getting worked up about its own tail.

"What's this?" I asked, gesturing at the dishes laid out on the counter.

"All for you," she said. "Hungry?"

I was hungry but unwilling to give her my gratitude.

"I worked on it all afternoon," she added.

"You shouldn't have," was my response.

Although the steaming food regarded me with rancor, my mother was still smiling. "I made this for you."

"Right."

Her face dropped.

"It's graduation week," I said. "You know that. I'm meeting friends. For dinner."

She seemed surprised that I was unable to appreciate her efforts. "Why not meet them later, for drinks? Here"—she dipped a spoon into the peanut sauce and brought it to my mouth—"taste this and tell me I don't love you."

I pushed her hand away from my face. "You don't love me."

A world of possibilities folded itself up, collapsed, vanished. If each relationship has one particular moment, of triumph or humiliation, of sudden insight or unbearable pain, that can flip the balance, this would have been it for us. Saying the words as though I meant them, I had screwed up, big time, in an unforgivable way. I knew it even before she turned her back on me as if on the devil.

She had it coming, of course, my rejection wasn't unjustified, but we were both disappointed by my failure to rise above her limitations. The small door she had opened, I had slammed shut. And worse: On a deep, dark level of my mind, I marveled at myself for having dared to do something so revengefully defiant.

I stir and blend and scrape. Frenetically.

Later in life, when regret chased the sleep from my nights, I reminded myself that I had never shown my mother the research I'd accumulated on the effects of cocaine on a fetus's undeveloped brain. I used to think it was my back-up. If my mother ever blamed me for my hostility, I could wave the report in my defense.

Cocaine use during pregnancy can induce a long-lasting disruption of dopamine receptors in the brain cells of the unborn, which alters the child's later ability to function. Common cognitive impairments are attention deficits, disorientation, mental confusion, self-animosity, night-mares, sexual disturbances, depersonalization, changed self-perception, learning disabilities, amnesia, emotional blunting and / or emotional hiccups.

Today at her grave, I wanted to believe that I'd concealed the report to spare her.

I set the dinner table for two with Delft Blue porcelain, good linen, real silverware—stuff that's only hauled out of the cupboard on special occasions of which I can only remember the one I refused to attend.

I light the candles, thinking of my mother as fearless. An old friend of hers at the funeral told me that she'd accepted the speed of her demise, but not the form in which it had arrived. So typical. Her cancer wasn't lifestyle-related, my mother had said, so her death was undeserved.

CABIN ON THE FAR SHORE

FRANCES BADGETT

Day 1

Your kayak, a hollow yellow crayon, slides past, tickle of eel grass, gentle current, your life in its hull. This is how you leave, a press away from the shore and silent hoist, current lap and sun-blind.

The afternoon is not everything, it is just light, cottonwood fluff, French press smash against the grounds. Sea plunge, a cormorant's sleek iridescence in the sun. Your voice carries over the breeze, then fails. I close my eyes and your afterimage is you against the sun, the sun against you. Your back, hat upturned, light rising hot and white.

The deck burns my bare feet. The seals wallow and splash. A wave breaks against a rock, and I think first it is a whale and second you, upturned. It is just a rock.

The squirrel you fed roots among the cool ferns, climbs the Doug you once hit with the car, drunk. Your eyes locked on an argument in your head. Things to stow.

I stack ice into a glass, pour water. Watch the ice crack and melt, the glass sweating on the counter. You used to say "There is nothing like ice water." There is nothing like a lot of things.

Day 2

The boy at the boathouse can't remember your name. You will dissolve in the heat, piece-by-piece, from memory after memory. I smile and thank him for the paddle and vest.

I tell myself I am not going out to find you. I keep close to the shore, our familiar shoals. Mussels cling in the surf, foam around the rocks.

I also tell myself that the boy who can't remember you knows my name, could never forget it. No one forgets. And then I know you are already pressing me into a book of memories like a wildflower. Dry, stiff, flat, lost.

Day 3

When they call, they speak so quietly I make them repeat it. You have never overshot a shoreline, never missed a dock, never steered wrong in a storm. This distant saltwater cabin you dreamed of every night while tossing next to the heat and breath of me will never hold you. You will never roll out the single mattress, damp with mildew. You will never unpack your one pot, the single wooden spoon. You had yelled once these were the only things you needed, angry with me for all my objects, shells from the beach, the crock pot.

I am remembering your mouth when you yell, the hollow sound of your stomps when you're angry. The eagle watches over the bay, as if you might come back today. In a day or so. Maybe now. You won't. The voice tells me they found your body resting against driftwood. The bright blur of your jacket in the surf.

The squirrel waits for you on the path to the water, alert and quivering. I hand him a peanut, his wary small paws reluctant.

Day 4

I fell asleep to your voicemail from the last day, milk and steaks for the grill, leaving so soon, you said, but we should have dinner first. We should mark our goodbye.

The need to be alone ate you until you were.

Year 1

I feed a squirrel. I think it could be yours, who knows. The calm water is glass, is flat. I load up a picnic and water and glide out. You aren't here. The water tells me what time is like. How pointless these hours. My legs numb under the stillness. The pills do their work, my limps slacken and fall. I have lost the paddle when they pull me out, drifting toward dark. Night fills the windows by the time I cool my sunburn against the sheets. My heart beats in my ears, too alive for me. All night in my dreams I am paddling after you, after the halo of sun and hat-tilt of you, rising over the next swell.

HOW TO BE MUGGED

JESSICA PIERCE

Open-palmed, my heart my heart my heart.
Am I speaking politely enough, giving
enough? Will I ever get up from
this sidewalk? So many hands. None
of them my own. My pulse has never been
so loud in my throat, my spine,
my fingertips. The men leave. I cry for
my mother. Name, address, what
was taken, name, address, what was taken.
All night, someone is coming.
No one is coming. I want to get up. I want
to breathe, clench my fists and run
until I kick against the sky, quenching
my thirst with my own sweat, my body mine
my body mine my body mine.

BEHIND THE SCENES

MONICA DICKSON

Continuity

She sees him every day. He goes home to his girlfriend every day. He tells her he loves her. He tells his girlfriend he loves her. When they're together they act like a couple. They are a couple.

Error in Geography

She lives in the city. He lives in the sticks. He tells his girlfriend that he's in the city, working. He is in the city but he's not working, he's going down on the girl who lives in the city but isn't his girlfriend. Except, like, now when she feels like she kinda is.

Locations

Places to meet are limited. She works at the Natural History Museum, looking after the stuffed bird display. He works in an office nearby but has a taxidermiphobia. One day he manages to overcome his fear and they have sex in the storecupboard known as "the breakout room."

Classic Quotes

She says: "The real thing is always more alluring than a plastic or digital version."
He says: "I can't think of anything more unnatural than a stuffed, dead bird on a plinth."

Cameo

She doesn't know his girlfriend; she's only seen a picture on his phone. But it turns out she went to school with his girlfriend's cousin. The cousin sees him, with her, in the city and puts two and two together.

Revealing Mistakes

The girl in the city, who thought she was his girlfriend, really—more so than his actual, official girlfriend—has made a mistake. She thought that because she didn't know his girlfriend in the sticks and because he made her sound like a bit of a wimp, that maybe she wasn't real, except in a hypothetically wimpy kind of way. She was wrong. The girlfriend in the sticks is really real and clever and funny and has a lot of good points to make, including that the boyfriend is a lying prick and that taxidermi-phobia is a surprisingly restrictive attribute and possibly, in his case, an affectation.

Director Trademark

The now ex-boyfriend has blocked them both on social media and refuses to answer their calls-slash-texts.

General Trivia

The girl from the city and the girl from the sticks have far more in common than either of them had with their former not-really boyfriend. They keep in touch and occasionally Snapchat if one of them spots a stuffed animal: a barn owl, mid-flight, ensnared behind glass; a wall-mounted stag's head, potent and pointless; a waistcoated fox, preserved on hind legs, proffering a drinks tray.

Anachronism

The practice of taxidermy is a throwback to Victorian times that can also be seen upon visiting a stately home or, perhaps more typically, when down at the traditional pub.

2019

Crazy Credits

The girl from the city and the girl from the sticks agree it is impossible to be in an exclusive relationship with two people at the same time, which is to say, simultaneously.

Disclaimer

No real, living creatures were ~~harmed mistreated~~ stuffed in the making of this story.

HOW TO BE YOUR MOTHER'S BEST DAUGHTER

YASMINA DIN MADDEN

1. Be humble, don't ask for too much, and don't ask questions.
2. Wear the French blouses with cap sleeves edged in lace when all the other girls dress in mini-skirts and paint-spattered sweatshirts slung from their shoulders.
3. Nod your head, but remain silent when she curses your father, your sisters, on the very rare occasion your brother...
4. Later, remain silent when she curses you.
5. Don't ask her what she means when she says you or your siblings 'don't have enough Asian.'
6. Study yourself in the mirror, though you suspect that what you look like has nothing to do with the Asian-ness your mother is after.
7. When she calls you during college, just say yes when she asks if you're being moral. If you must, let the phone dangle from its cord and go into the hallway to talk with your friends. She will still be talking when you return.
8. Try to understand that she means well.
9. Don't have the third glass of wine at dinner with her, even if you really want it.
10. Visit her at least three times a year and when you do, fetch the green onions from the crisper, the rice from the pantry, slice the pork belly, chop the onions, dice the peppers, stir the soup.

11. Request the recipe.
12. Watch her curl her hand into a loose fist and bat it against her legs when she gets nervous.
13. Remember watching your grandmother, her mother, do the exact same thing while pacing the confines of a small one-room apartment on the outskirts of Paris.
14. Tell your husband not to be alarmed when, after your wedding vows conclude, your mother hugs him tight and whispers in his ear, "I ask only one thing: Never get divorced."
15. Do not, under any circumstances, get divorced.
16. If you decide to have children, don't be offended when she says she needs only three things from you:
    a. That the child be given a normal name (your father's*)
    b. That the child is baptized.
    c. And, finally, that the child is circumcised.*
    *If it's a girl, replace your father's name with your grandmother's and subtract circumcision.
17. Nod your head, but remain silent, when she tells you not to compliment your child too much.
18. Continue to compliment your child, but more quietly.
19. Remember that your mother waited in America, at the tail end of a war between her new home and the country of her childhood, wondering what would become of her own mother, who walked through jungles and crossed oceans to survive.
20. Watch her eyes fill with tears when she knows you or one of your siblings is in pain. Watch her lips press together, open, press together again.
21. Let her fill your plate, fill it again, and yet one more time, even if you are full.
22. Believe her when she tells you food is love.
    a. Remember that it takes hours and hours to make Chả giò, and that she makes it, your favorite, without the help of her own sisters who live thousands of miles away on another continent.

    b. Agree that this is the kind of food that calls for the hands of many to prepare it.

23. Listen, listen, listen as she laments over the various ways in which she's suffered.

24. Keep listening.

WHEN THE ALIENS ARRIVE THEY WILL CUT OFF OUR WIFI

KELSEY IPSEN

T he first time I see the UFO is via a 10-second video on twitter. It is a shaky, blinking light against the hurried ink of the sky. With the sound off you don't hear the group of people behind the camera swearing. 'Pretty. I wish the aliens would visit us every night,' my daughter says. She is six and she believes in everything because she has no reason not to. She asks to watch the video again and again until it is her bedtime. When I go to brush my teeth I hear the soft squeaking of her bed. She is standing on her mattress, fingertips smudging the window, staring into the sky.

I'm at work and my husband sends me an article about the UFO. There are a series of photos and videos showing the light getting bigger. ':o' I reply. 'Don't tell Sarah :p' comes his answer. But when I get home they are both on Sarah's bed. My husband has bought a telescope and they are taking turns looking through the lens. 'What do the aliens eat?' Sarah asks. My husband looks at me like what do aliens eat? But I don't have an answer. 'Probably something we've never heard of.' He decides. It is now my turn to look through the lens and I watch the light turn off and on and off and on. 'They don't eat humans?' Sarah asks. 'Would you eat something you had never seen, especially if that thing was walking and talking?' I say. 'Ew no,' says Sarah, and I hope the aliens are a little bit like her.

When the light gets closer nobody has any signal, we guess this is because the UFO is blocking all the waves. We don't panic because we do not read about other people's panic. We don't tell the world how much we love each other, we tell ourselves. Again, and again, and again. I get the idea that we might all die. My husband points out that it will be less sad if we all die together and I imagine no one missing anyone, ever, and I think that he must be right.

On the street everyone is looking up, the outlines of their phones visible through their pockets. Their hands are hooked instead around their own hands or around the hands of others. There is a man a few streets over who has taken to shouting about the end of the world but we just change our route home. I guess that somewhere there are humans moving underground. I guess that somewhere there are humans downing poison. I guess that there are millions freaking out and planning their last words, but we have Sarah who delights in the arrival, who loves the aliens before they even touch the ground. Her attitude is contagious. I keep hearing her say 'Pretty.' It's a pleasure to enjoy the real world. We stay up late and tell stories about how we imagine the aliens to be. Sometimes they are green, sometimes they speak through their hands touching ours or though their minds transmitting ideas directly into our human brains. Sometimes they are just thoughts in floating orbs or beams of fractured light. We imagine these things and more, as the light from the ship illuminates us then plunges us into darkness as it spins.

We camp out by the window in Sarah's room. We don't want to take our eyes off what is happening. The ship is massive, we can see the bones of it now through the glare. It makes no noise, when not looking up you can't tell anything is really happening. 'I guess I always imagined it would be loud.' Says my husband and I nod. A car screams down the street, a man clutching the wheel so tight I can see the effort it takes him from where I'm sitting. 'We are the loud ones.' Says Sarah, and we have to agree with her. 'Maybe they came all the way here, across millions of galaxies, to tell us to shut up.' I say and Sarah laughs, like this is the funniest idea in the whole universe. My husband and I do not laugh because we have seen the ship opening. An assortment of aliens disembark and we wait. I feel my husband's body next to me, tensed as if ready to run, whether it would be towards or away from the aliens I do not know. Sarah looks up, wiping tears from her eyes, just in time to see the aliens raise their fingers in unison and put them to their lips.

THE GRAND AM

TYLER BARTON

His mother said a good cry grew in your gut—a bad cry, in your brain. She'd always fail to calm him by insisting there was a difference. Don't worry, Lovey, this is a good one. Good cries held a glass of wine, a book face down across the thigh. A good cry wore proper shoes: fuzzy socks with rubber floor grips. A good cry involved the dog, regal, sitting tall beside her, an ivory thing she reached for, to steady herself, a cane.

Bad cries were things she hid. They happened in the Pontiac. Driver's seat. 9:45 pm. Just home from work. Headlights off. Seatbelt still buckled. He'd watch her from the window beside his pillow. Down there. Where the only light was the winking red eye of the Marlboro. How it shook in her hand. Grand-Am filling with smoke. When she finally crept inside, he was as bad at feigning sleep as she was at pretending to believe him.

Tonight—his stomach growling, blood pulsing in both temples—he wants to call her. Not to apologize, not to answer the question of why he never calls, but to ask for a diagnosis. Mom, listen. Tell me which this is.

RUTHLESSLY, DENYING

TOMMY DEAN

Veronica stood inside the closet and pushed the hangers back and forth, the rattle of plastic, a distraction from the horror film that privately played through her mind. Cady's death was a thing so bizarre as to be laughable had it happened in a movie. Fuck was the only word to describe her grief and until now she was too afraid to say it out loud. She stepped out of the closet, hands on her hips, and said, "Just what the fuck am I supposed to wear?"

Russ cringed, and the beer tipped off his stomach and onto the bed. The liquid pooled around him before settling into the sheet and then the mattress. Scooping up the can, he jumped out of the bed. Veronica hoped he'd say something, but he stood there next to the bed, the heavy suck of breath coming in and out of his nose as he tried not to cry. She knew he was just as devastated as she was, but she wanted to wreck him, the way she felt every time she saw one of those Rockwell paintings. She walked around the edge of the bed and put her hand on his shoulder and he shuddered like a semi braking hard on a short yellow light.

"Don't. Okay?" he said. "Just don't."

She didn't know if he meant the cussing or the touching. If she had a can-opener, she'd crank open his skull and wait for his thoughts to spill out on the floor between them.

"Russ, I'll take care of it. Everything," she said, dropping her hand to the edge of the sheet.

"Leave it. I'll just sleep on the couch. I can't take any comfort in it anyway. I deserve a whole lot worse."

Veronica hated the way he could take the air out of her anger, popping the balloon rising in her chest, by saying the things she wanted to say. It left her unsettled, unsure of what to say next, especially when she wasn't sure she was done trying to hurt him. Their marriage didn't use to thrive on hurt, but the pain from Cady's death was like an autoimmune disease, targeting her very cells, prodding them until they were about to burst.

"Give me five minutes and you can come back and lay down. Half of it's your bed too."

"Forget it," he said. "I'll go check on the truck." He sucked in his snot like a child, the sound stopping them both, each of them thinking of Cady, the things she would no longer do.

Veronica shook out the new sheet, the fabric billowing up between them. When it fell twisted onto the bed, Russ was standing in the doorway, hands braced against the wood, his back to her, speaking into the other room. "I've seen people do this in the movies. The man who is so overcome he can't make it out of the room. I thought it was so fake, so Hollywood, but I get it now. Like those runners who crawl across the finish line. I never understood that level of exhaustion."

She can't touch him, can't punch him, can't scream, she promised herself that she was done with that. She bent over the bed, the smell of beer too close to her face for comfort, but she fussed with the corner, pulling it tight around the end of the mattress until he left, his steps heavy on the laminate floors. She refused to follow him, thinking that they both deserved their own spaces, not knowing if this more than the act of the death itself would break them.

When she got to the last corner, the sheet bunched in her hand, refusing to move forward. She put the sheet on the wrong way and she would have to start over. She rarely got it right on the first try, but those small domestic hang-ups found the dark center of her grief and anger, each one another indignity. She ripped the sheet off and flipped it into the air, trying to settle it correctly this time, the fabric billowing, like a single tawny cloud, so round, like Cady's cheeks. This was the difference for a mother, every goddamn thing reminded you of your children. Physical pictures were for the other family members, mother's had images and snippets of videos that ran through their consciousness, waiting in the background of their minds like landmines, popping up and exploding at the most unreasonable times, without the slightest provocation.

"Fuck," she said, the sheet falling to the bed, wrinkled and lifeless. They wouldn't break, she thought. They'd weather together, beat to hell by their grief, where they'd find shelter in each other or they'd erode slowly like islands awaiting the water rushing over their shores until the only evidence of their marriage existed in pictures—like maps of forgotten cities.

2020

STAR COUNT OF ORION

CAROLIENA CABADA

One long night in December, Orion—yes that Orion—was my lover.
We met at a diner. Orion waved away the cream that came with his coffee carafe. He took his coffee black, and said that milk was like a crude street lamp leaking artificial light into something pristine.

He was a bit mean, but I was drawn to him anyway. Like I was lost at sea and he was there, taking up the whole sky to help me navigate safely.

When we got back to my place, I tried to stay up all night. I ate caffeine pills when I ran out of coffee grounds, black tea, and chocolate-covered espresso beans. But on my last cup of budget-brand dark roast, he shook his head and laughed when I added in a few drops of half-and-half.

I didn't have a plan of seduction. In general, I am drawn to liquids and warmth, and so I thought he might be the same. Of the soups I could make on my single burner—condensed cream of mushroom, condensed chicken noodle, condensed beef stew—he didn't have a preference.

But we took our bowls out onto the balcony in the below-zero weather. Polar night of an Arctic winter. I could only handle about five minutes of the cold, even with my many layers and the hot soup burning its way down my throat. Orion stood out there for hours, looking for his place in the sky. The soup froze.

We had the rest of the night, and we took it. He told me to turn off the lights, close the blinds and the curtains. I found another blanket to cover the window. In the blackout, he was bright like alarm clock numbers at three in the morning.

Only he was bright that way everywhere. At the tips of his elbows. All across his freckled nose. Luminescent eyelashes. Fingernails. Happy trail. He tasted like good espresso and felt like a first wish—sincere and deep.

He told me, in our afterglow, that he was wandering because he was fading. There was too much light in and out of the city. When I woke up at polar twilight, pink horizon at the edge of a navy blue sky, he was gone. And he didn't return when true dark fell again.

Now I drive incessantly. City to prairie to mountain. Arctic to Antarctic. I avoid the midnight sun. Every time I stop, I look up and count the stars inside the four corners of that body; less than ten and he's not really there. I burn fuel to move and linger on the three pins of his belt.

PLAY PRETEND

EMILY CEMENTINA

why
do I
crave
home
remembering
it
like some
oasis

not sure
it ever was

though
yes
sunlight

afternoons
with
floral dresses

the
whole yard

my kingdom

2020

I
do
recall
greenery
a prick
turned
to softness

how
a rock
could cool you

this
alone
made me

majestic

NOW

MARC DARNELL

Hug your son and tell him you love him,
or do something with him, anything—
stop tinkering with your crap in the garage.

That overgrown toolshed isn't an homage
to the greasy god of car part hoarding.
Hug your son and tell him you love him.

In a few more years he won't be driven
to sleep in the house of a widower drinking.
Stop tinkering with your crap. In the garage

the yellowed calendar girls know your age—
you can't sit on the beach with them mingling,
so hug your son. Tell him you love him

before your headlights are cracked and dim,
while he's in a far place, his heart sinking,
and you're still tinkering in the garage

as you gasp with acid reflux and wage
war with esophageal cancer, and start thinking
it's too late to find him and tell him you love him
before they bury you under your crap in the garage.

SKYWATCH

JESSIE LOVETT ALLEN

They're probably not real, but Faye asks just to be sure. And she is surprised that daddy says yes, witches are real, except they don't have green faces, pointy black hats, or an army of flying monkeys. They look regular, like everyone. "Now go to sleep." He leaves the bedroom, and it feels like a rubber hammer is hitting her stomach and sending tingles out to her limbs. Like that time she accidentally touched the horse's carrot to the electric fence. Witches could be living in the apartment complex, swimming in their pool, and using the washer and dryer in the basement.

Sunnie is already asleep beside her in the double bed. "Sunnie!" she whispers. Her sister's eyes stay closed, but she can feel the cool skin from Sunnie's foot on her calf.

In the morning, she and Sunnie walk through the piles of fallen leaves to find the longest sticks in the park. Then, they find the deepest puddles, poke the tips of the sticks into the puddles, and hold them still. This is fishing. Their stick-poles hold invisible strings that descend into an invisible ocean, under the puddle, full of giant goldfish, friendly dolphins, and maybe even a mermaid.

***

They move to a house, and Faye no longer shares a bedroom with Sunnie. Every night, lights beam through the window, shining up the entire bedroom. Yes, her house is across from the stop sign of an intersection, but this seems far too bright for just headlights, and she's sure it's the rapture.

This is it: Jesus has descended from heaven, and within moments all the believers will be sucked up to heaven like in the pictures of the children's bible book. She holds her breath, and then the shadows slowly float across the wall as the car turns right.

Sometimes, on bad nights, even after she is too old for it, she calls out for her mother who will squeeze into the twin bed. Mom's breath is warm. "I'm afraid of dying," she'll say. And her mom, meaning well, tells her that there's nothing to fear because she had accepted Jesus into her heart, so she would live forever in heaven. But this is no comfort because eternal life in heaven—for infinity—terrifies her.

"When do you think Jesus will come back?" she asks.

"I don't know," mom says. "No man knows the hour, no man knows the day. That's what the Bible says." Once, though, her mom had admitted that she, personally, felt the rapture was long overdue and thought it would've happened in the seventies. After a while her mother's warmth, at first comforting, feels stifling.

"You can go back to your bed," she assures her mom. "I'm OK now."

It all seems silly in the morning when she's eating a Pop Tart, but somehow every night Christ's return seems more plausible than a driver pausing for 30 seconds at the stop sign while fumbling for his glasses in the center console.

* * *

After freshman year Comparative Religion class, the rapture seems a lot less scary than that Fire in Sky movie, totally based on a true story of alien abduction, in which a regular dude is just riding home with his friends and a column of light sucks him up into an alien spaceship. The aliens keep him for a few days, encased in slime, except for when they take him out to poke a giant needle into his eyeball. Then he wakes up naked, shivering, and incoherent outside a gas station in the middle of the night. In real life, this dude and all the guys in the truck passed lie detectors.

Faye will take a hit from the bong and laugh and joke to her friends, "Aliens scare the SHIT out of me!" But at 3:45 AM, it's no joke. On summer nights, she'll sleep with the rickety window propped open, and the cool, humid breeze will swirl inside the apartment. Noises will wake her: maybe the downstairs neighbor, drunk and yelling in the alley, or the jangle of the blinds sucked against the window. She imagines the scene in the movie.

Needle in the eyeball.

Needle in the eyeball.

Neptune, a black cat who belonged to a former roommate, leaps up near her face, purring, and digs at the sheet, burrowing a tunnel down to her feet.

* * *

After the baby comes, there is no headspace left for these sadistic aliens. The nebulizer whirrs as Faye tries to keep the baby-sized gas mask over his mouth and nose. After the breathing treatment, his breaths settle deeper and quieter. She passes in and out of sleep with a hand on his chest, feeling it crest in tiny waves. She dreams that he slips from her hands into a murky pond, and this jolts her awake, splashing through the sheets like water. He's there in the bassinet. Not submerged, not sinking. But the way the nightlight casts a shadow, his profile looks like an alien.

It is winter, so in the daytime they walk inside malls, past soft pretzels, Hot Topics, and tiled fountains. When the baby fusses, she rolls the stroller to the hallway off the food court near the Panda Express where there's a special room for nursing mothers. The rocking chairs are made with durable upholstery, the type that a custodian can spray with a sanitizing solution and wipe clean with a rag. As she nurses the boy under the fluorescent lights, she thinks of all the mothers who have held their babies in this chair, and then all the mothers in the city who are nursing their babies right now, and how mothers are nursing babies at other malls in Montana in Indiana and all over the world in yurts and fields and slums and luxury hotels above oceans and deserts.

* * *

The baby becomes a boy who can reach the top pantry shelf. The boy jumps off docks and splashes into lakes. At night, he tools around on back roads. It is on one of these nights that she realizes she is becoming invisible. Once, years ago, Sunnie had asked Faye which superpower she would prefer: invisibility or flying? According to Sunnie, this question was supposed to reveal something essential about you, and people are pretty much split fifty-fifty in how they answer. Faye couldn't—and still cannot—imagine why anyone would choose invisibility, unless they're a pervert or a robber. But Sunnie disagreed. "What a relief it would be," Sunnie had said, Like, parallel to the world, but no pressure." Sunnie sat on the porch swing with a cold glass bottle of Diet Rite between her thighs.

"Invisibility shouldn't even be a superpower," Faye had said.

But Faye is resilient, and so she wills herself to see this involuntary invisibility as an asset. She tries shoplifting, which turns out to be easy when you're invisible. She starts with small items, like lip balm and Tic Tacs, but when you're invisible you can also walk out with big lawn chairs, curtain rods, and bags of bird seed. But in the parking lot afterwards, the parallel dimension feels lonely and frightening, so she quits stealing.

Instead she pays hundreds of dollars for needles in her forehead and around her mouth that paralyze and plump and slow down the creep of invisibility, at least a little. She's not afraid of these needles; she welcomes them. They hardly hurt. When the dermatologist has other doctors-in-training job shadow at the office, he asks if it's OK for them to watch the procedure. "Of course," she says warmly. "I'd like to welcome you all to my Botox," she jokes. And they all laugh, and they observe carefully how the doctor inserts the needle and pushes the syringe.

* * *

When the boy is a man who leases a Toyota Camry, Faye wakes with an aching bladder, certain that everyone she loves will inevitably die. And of course they will. But she only feels this truth in her stomach when it's 4:00 AM and she's sitting on her toilet with Santa fleece pajama pants around her ankles. This clarity thrives in that liminal space between sleep and awake, between consciousness and oblivion.

People, of course, really do get raptured every day. Sometimes it's a fast rapture, like a car accident or septic shock, or a slow rapture, like how Sunnie had the kind of cancer that seemed to go away but metastasized in the brain three years later. She's too logical to worry about plane crashes and other cliché nonsense. Choking on a piece of steak while eating at home alone is a far more plausible scenario. What would that be like? Maybe you would dial 9-1-1, but you couldn't say anything into the phone. Maybe you would look up a video online about how to do the Heimlich maneuver on yourself, and it would probably have an ad you'd have to watch before the tutorial started.

No, this isn't anxiety—anxiety is defined by uncertainty. But she is certain. If it's not the steak, it'll be a grape or a Gobstopper or a bratwurst. And if it isn't choking it'll be a wipeout on the concrete steps or an aortic aneurysm. She knows that anxiety lies and makes you worry about things unlikely to happen, but this feeling is no liar because these worries will become reality. Eventually. This feeling is more like anticipatory grief.

One morning when she can't fall back asleep, she wraps herself in the quilt and steps out to the porch. It is dark, but there's a haze of dawn at the edge of the purple sky. Although most of the stars have faded, she can still see two bright planets. An army of cranes, advancing north for spring, are flying low enough that she can hear them squawk and warble. The cold air swirls at her legs where the pajama pants don't reach.

And Faye remembers Sharla, who'd worked in the cafeteria. Sharla would stock the salad bar during the lunch rush, but her legs grew stiff and swollen from circulation problems, so they let her move to register and sit on a stool. One day Sharla was gone. Dead. Probably heart failure, they said. But she'd overheard another cafeteria worker explaining how it happened: Sharla was playing cards at a friend's house with a group of ladies, and she'd seemed just fine, and her husband came to pick her up, and only when they pulled into their own driveway did he discover that she had died, right there in the passenger's seat.

Faye imagines Sharla's husband, gently steadying her by the elbow as she slides into the front seat. Soft music on the car radio. A vibrant sunset visible out the windshield.

SPINSTER, SHREW, HARRIDAN

AMY KIGER-WILLIAMS

What kind of woman would I be if I didn't define myself by the boyfriends in my life? Would I be the kind of woman who knew how to change a flat tire? Would I hang drywall in my apartment with a few other women friends? Would we make it a party, drink cabernet sauvignon and eat some Brie that I picked up at Whole Foods and placed on a makeshift table consisting of a small scrap of plywood and an upside-down spackling bucket, because we would be inventive women who built walls where walls didn't exist before and created everything out of nothing and didn't need boyfriends to help us with anything, even finding a proper surface for our party foods? Would I be able to swap out a malfunctioning electrical socket with a brand-new model that wouldn't catch fire? Would I do all of the things that I sometimes wait for a boyfriend to do, or sometimes call a contractor who becomes (or hopes to become) a boyfriend, who might stay around for a little while because God forbid my apartment catches fire, or my walls fall inward on each other, crushing my party table? What would happen if my AAA membership lapses, leaving me and my deflated tire alone, stranded by the side of the highway, waiting for another boyfriend to come and help hoist the car up on the jack?

What kind of woman would I be if I could hoist the car up on the jack?

What kind of woman would I be if I didn't feel alone without a warm body next to me in the bed? Would I fall asleep easily? Would I still take

Ambien? Would a dog help? Would it have to be a large dog, or would a little pup suffice? How about a cat? Would a cat actually make me look like the sort of woman who couldn't get a boyfriend? Would I be a spinster? A shrew? A harridan?

What is a harridan, anyway?

What kind of woman would I be if I considered the idea of spending my hours not being a woman who is waiting to catch fire with a boyfriend who tells me he likes the arrangement like this, the way that no one knows about us, as if we are a sweet, horrible secret, or a second boyfriend, who doesn't love me at all, who is using me, my women friends tell me over wine and a cheese plate, who borrows money sometimes when he runs short on the 28th of the month, then forgets that he had just borrowed money when the 1st of the month rolls around, his bank account newly plump again, who wants me to take his dog for a while, since he can't afford him, for Christ's sake! or a third boyfriend who got mad at me for being me and called me a spinster, a shrew, and a harridan, who I see driving past my apartment, past my job, past the Walgreens when I'm picking up my monthly supply of Ambien, past the restaurant where I'm having dinner with the first or second boyfriend, past my car in the Home Depot parking lot where I have parked because I have decided to become a woman who can swap out a malfunctioning electrical socket, a woman who can put up a wall with the help of her cabernet-drinking, Brie-eating friends? What would happen if right at that moment, I notice that my car's left rear tire, the one resting on a yellow line in the Home Depot parking lot, is flat, goddamn it, and the third boyfriend sees his chance, and he steps out of his car that he's parked threateningly behind mine and says with a fake smile in his voice, "Hey, funny seeing you here, do you need a hand?" What kind of person am I when I think about how I don't want to be a woman stranded by the side of a highway, or in a Home Depot parking lot, or ever, ever a woman at the mercy of a man's help, and I smile with all of the teeth in my mouth so he won't get angry at me for being me, and I say, "No, thank you, I've got this?"

What are the walls that I am building where no walls existed before when I decide to create everything out of nothing?

Who am I when I realize that I don't need a boyfriend to help me with anything?

And what kind of woman am I in that very moment when I finally reach into the trunk of my car and I pull out the jack?

A BLACK MAMA'S BREATHWORK OR, THE FIRST TIME I HAD "THE TALK" WITH MY DAUGHTER

DW MCKINNEY

I (inhaled, then) exhaled pain into my daughter's hair. It wasn't my plan. My husband was supposed to be sitting in my place, his legs open, a red plastic chair squeezed between them with our four-year-old sitting atop the seat. And while he moisturized and detangled her curly puff ponytail, I was going to sit in our bedroom closet, lights off and body hugged against the stinking laundry bag, to weep. But plans, like they tend to, changed. And so I sat with *my* legs open, wide-tooth comb in one hand and a spray bottle in the other, and (inhaled, then) exhaled pain into my daughter's hair.

I (inhaled, then) exhaled and said, "You know about the virus, right? [She nodded and said yes.] Well, there's other things going on too." I inhaled thinking that would stop whatever it was I was going to say, the damage I was about to do. I held my breath and imagined my father sitting next to me as he inhaled the world and exhaled, "You know your ABCs right? [I did.] But do you know 'em backwards? See, baby, you gotta be prepared because some cop'll pull you over and have you saying the ABCs backward, trying to trip you up and haul your ass off to jail." And I remembered his angry, raggedy breathing as we recited the ABCs backward as we sat on the living room couch, and as he drove us in his Volvo down the highway and he asked me to keep an eye out for the police, and as we sat in the car later eating ice cream from Thrifty's.

I exhaled that memory and more pain came out of me than I wanted. I breathed a fraught life into existence and it nestled in my daughter's curls. I had to get it out of me, of her. More than anything, I just wanted to get out of here—this world. "People are marching in the street. They're angry. [She asked why people were angry.] Some people out there hate Mama's skin." And because folks on the Internet, doctors and psychologists, said parents should be *specific* when informing their children, I (inhaled, then) exhaled my pain into the ragged parts I had made in my daughter's hair with the rat-tail comb and *specifically* cut the innocence from her throat as I said, "People hate Mama's skin because she's Black. I'm Black. You know you're Black, too, right? [She nodded and asked which people hated me. Was it the bad people?] Yes, the bad people." Then she wondered if it was the bad people we saw on the bus. Before the virus, we'd always see the black and white bus taking "bad guys" to the local lock-up by our house. These were the bad guys she knew. They probably looked like cartoons in her mind. I couldn't quite tell her that some of those bad people were also driving the bus and running the lock up. But it didn't matter. Bad guys wanted to hurt Mama. And bad guys wanted to hurt her.

Then my daughter (inhaled, then) exhaled pain too. I held my breath when she said she'd protect me. She'd beat up the bad guys. I didn't say a word. Couldn't. I didn't want to cut more of that innocence from her throat. "Thank you," I said and kept (inhaling, then exhaling and) combing and twisting her hair.

And so while my white husband was upstairs in the rocking chair, cradling our youngest daughter, cradling her sleepy head with ease, without the pain of running into closets to weep into a pile of dirty laundry, I was downstairs with our oldest daughter. The both of us inhaled and exhaled pain in silence as we stared out at the sheet of night beyond the sliding glass window, our bodies rigid, our hair parted.

FRUIT

LISA BASS

After Hicok

"There was this moment where I was like, 'Oh shit, I ate *six* of them,'" Persephone said to Ira Glass. She let out an incredulous laugh, throatier than I'd have thought.

"I was leaning against this rock outside the throne room. It's kind of my spot?" She said it like a question and Ira Glass made "mmhmmm"ing noises in assent.

"I had this pomegranate in my hand," Persephone said.

"*The* pomegranate?" asked Ira Glass.

"Well, yeah. I was looking at those pathways of seeds," said Persephone. "You know how if you look at something long enough, it stops being what it is and becomes something else entirely?"

Ira Glass said he knew exactly, like how you sometimes get stuck staring in the mirror at the place where your nose runs into the rest of your face. I glanced at my reflection in the window above the kitchen sink: I was distorted under the recessed lighting, just broad strokes of myself.

"I was thinking how those rows of seeds look like veins," Persephone said, "when I felt that current along my neck that meant the souls were gathering."

"Wait, what?" said Ira Glass.

"They never came too close. Mostly, they'd cluster against the atrium wall."

"You're talking about what's left of dead people? Spirits?" asked Ira Glass.

"Honestly, they'd been creeping me out for weeks," said Persephone. "When I sensed them, I'd pretend to look through them, like they weren't there."

"Wow," said Ira Glass.

"But this time, I don't know. Something was different." Her voice got quiet, reverent. I turned off the faucet so I wouldn't miss anything.

"I really saw them," she said. "Their faces were just there, translucent, looking right at me."

"Were you freaking out?" asked Ira Glass.

"Their need was just so strong." Music started playing under Persephone's words, the rhythmic kind they put on to let us know that something meaningful is about to happen. "I felt like they really needed me. *Me*. Not the daughter. Not the girlfriend."

"They were seeing you for yourself," said Ira Glass.

"I mean, yeah. I hadn't even known I wanted that. But for the first time, I felt such purpose. So I did it. I lifted a seed to my mouth and bit into it. There was all this tart juice. It stung the inside of my cheeks."

"Wait," said Ira Glass. "This is crazy. I've always heard that you didn't realize what you were doing. Or that you were hungry." Ira Glass was excited, speaking quickly. The cracks in his voice were multiplying, like the warning crevices that sprawl across a fault zone.

"Ira, I swear, once I decided to go for it, those seeds floated right into my mouth."

"Are you serious?"

"Really. I pierced their little skins, one after another. Finally, I swallowed all six of them at once."

Ira Glass switched to voice-over mode, marveling that Persephone had *known* that eating the pomegranate would tether her to the Underworld. He told us that she had expected to feel a major change after she swallowed the pomegranate seeds, "but actually?" said Ira Glass, leaving charged pauses between his words, "She felt. Exactly. The same." It wasn't until months later, he explained, after days of tending souls, walking the river bank, not until well after the wedding that she understood what she had done.

"This one afternoon," Persephone said, "we'd just finished meeting with our last soul. I looked up, and there she was."

"Your mother," said Ira Glass.

"My mother." Persephone let out a staggered sigh. "Her hair used to be so coarse, and now, the individual strands were still thick, but there were so few of them. I was fixated on her scalp, on the white spaces between her hair." My breath caught at the waver in the goddess' voice.

"I wanted to take it back."

"To unswallow the pomegranate," Ira Glass said.

"I'd been gone all that time, and I hadn't even thought about my mother, about her need."

Ira Glass began analyzing what it's like when you realize your parents have grown old and I became lost in the rhythm of scrubbing the cast iron pan. I imagined that my hands were my mother's hands and they were my daughter's hands, all of us at once sifting the water through our outstretched fingers, lulled into an almost sleep, a river flowing about our necks and heads. I saw myself teaching my daughter to surf the rapids on a piece of driftwood without telling her that the current would take her too far downstream to ever make her way back; showing her how to avoid a turbulent eddy, but willing the panic out of my voice so she wouldn't tense up and tumble into the whitewater; pretending that if she could maneuver around this particular set of boulders, she'd be certain to keep her balance downriver on the more treacherous runs when I heard Persephone tell Ira Glass, "I kept trying to say something to ease this charged tension between us. My mouth would make the shapes, but no sound came." Ira Glass sighed, like he wanted to heal the cracks, like he wanted to keep what is fractured within us whole.

"We were almost to the gate when she got really still," Persephone said. "And her stillness flowed through me, it drew me to her. My head settled into the hollow of her shoulder."

Everything went quiet then, a heavy silence that held Persephone's longing.

I was reaching to check my headphone connection when Persephone finally said, "She would leave, I would stay. We both knew this. But first my mother whispered to me. She told me that we would have enough strength and enough love to hold all that is coming."

"That's lovely," said Ira Glass.

"Enough strength and enough love to sustain us," said Persephone, her voice growing faint; I strained to make out her words, "through our loss and our sorrow."

KELP FOREST

ANNA GATES HA

He sleeps next to me on the big bed, so I can nurse him without really waking up, although I am awake now, in the dark. I am always awake in the dark. The cat cleans herself at the edge of the bed, perks her ears, eyes flashing for a moment when my son's foot rustles under the white sheets. I think, how long can a person live without sleep before she disappears entirely? He rolls, again, cries to nurse.

In the morning, I will take him outside, underneath the lemon tree. I will kick away the rotting ones. We will smash a few of them with our feet, make them pop and ooze, and for me this will conjure the ocean—the sand littered with bulbous kelp covered in flies, how they would take flight as I jumped. The satisfaction in the pop. Of ripping something open, all the inside air escaping.

I will let him hold a hose until there is an entire muddy ocean underneath the lemon tree. He will make me count down from five, again and again and again, jumping when I get to blast off. He will start out in boots and shorts and a shirt, but by the end of it, because this is how it always goes, he will be down to his diaper, brown and bulging. I will be covered in little flecks of mud, and when I pick at a spot on my knee, he will notice, and want me covered completely, like him. He will come after me with muddy hands, and I will run away and scream, and he will love this, this chase, but I will be done by then, ready to clean him, ready for him to nap. I will end the game too sharply. Scold him when he doesn't stop. But he will not back down.

So I will sit beneath the lemon tree and let his hands cover me in mud, and if I close my eyes I will fall asleep, right here, and let my son and the sun mummify me in mud. Let it build and build, layer upon layer, and when he is finished covering me up, he might mistake me for a rotting lemon—or bulbous kelp, lost, a long way from home—from the purple urchins nibbling at my stock, the otters weaving through me, my foliage moving softly with tide, filtering the light—and maybe he will jump on me then, let me crack and delight in the pop, nothing but air escaping, bursting up quietly, softly, barely there at all.

ILLUSIONS CLOTHE

ELI GOLDBLATT

To cut thru things around us—this gentle
surgery always at hand, incited by scent or red
scarf or blue rough hand towel—not memory
alone nor lingering regret but a fresh trail in
faint snow, katsura leaf caught on a drying
weed stem, full moon yellowed on late
December horizon line. Fire sirens from
3 blocks away mark bright henna scars
across my cheek. Bribes & duplicity, anger

& hate: illusions clothe passengers on the
bus, cops patrolling the pitted avenue, even
a little trembling dog held in his ancient
owner's arms as they enter the Rite Aid
at Walnut Lane. Blankets & screens,
scaffolding & brackets, wheeled walkers
& carved canes. I look up at lights around
Vision Works, down at the slab lifted by
a curbside maple. I'm afraid of falling &

I fall into the cauldron dyeing heavy cotton
weave an iron orange, repeated figures

dance at the hem neither precious nor
coarse. I choose the middle path to govern
spirits when I cry out in dream, banishing
abandoned children from our rooms.

FRONTIER MOTHER

DAVON LOEB

The exterior was like the car had just driven through a sandstorm: rusted, chipped paint, exposed primer. There was one tire of a different size that replaced an original, so it wobbled off its axis. And you'd have to lick your fingers and twist a couple wires for the radio to work—the voices cutting on and off, from FM to AM to silence. The car needed struts. The car needed pads. The car needed blades for its wipers that left half-circles etched in the glass. And something black and tarry and thick that was reminiscent of motor oil dripped and had been following us from departure. But it ran, like how a smoker with emphysema ran. And you might not have been able to tell who was more broken—the car or her—how her hair was split and wrapped in something faded and frilly—and that the frames she only wore before bed magnified hot and puffy dark eyes, and that she pulled on whatever sweatpants and sweatshirt she could find in the closet—that her clothes didn't match, her perfumed wasn't sprayed, and she might not have showered at all. And while this does not define a broken woman, this woman was in pieces.

Like this car that sputtered, hissed, and wheezed; and when she continued forgetting to press the clutch, the gears ground, and we covered our ears, and the metal on metal sounded like two cars like two pulleys pushing into each other. Like us, crammed together in the backseat, my big sister and big brother and me, like a trio of nesting dolls, watching our mother become something else. For on a normal day, before all of this happened, before the rage, panic, and dishevelment, she was regal: double-breasted blazer, pleated pants, blouses begonia-bright and feathery-petaled soft. Our mother was planned, precise, purposeful, like the inside of an organizer. But now, still saying things under her upheaving chest, the rising and falling of breath as if she was still pacing around our house—still throwing whatever she could into her military-issued duffel: a sleeve of diapers, a pack of wipes, a set of Nancy Drews, a brigade of army men, a photo book, a manila envelope, handfuls of clothes, snacks in baggies, and her purse that dangled so heavily it welted her brown skin.

Maybe we were runaways. And this was after her divorce, but before she signed the papers, just when she left—when she had enough—that the lies had grown like a cancer grows and had spread from her heart throughout her body—how the lies were in the walls, how they were asbestos, how their home was poison, how the foundation had been eaten away, how it was not safe, how she couldn't take it a moment more. And while driving for however long on I-95, she imagined herself as a frontier woman in her caravan with her children, and that when she stepped on the gas it was like horses galloping on a dirt road, and that the billow of smoke was just the dust of tumbleweeds, and that the sun looked new now, an orange she'd never seen before, as if the insides of a grapefruit; and she thought it was the same sun some woman had seen when she moved westward, and that woman didn't need a husband either, that she could load that wagon, that she was as strong as she was fit a mother, and that in-between third and fourth gear now, she secured her left hand to the steering wheel and the right unfolded a map across the passenger seat, and her finger followed a route that she had traced in red marker the night before.

THE WEIGHT YOU KNOWINGLY CARRY

KATIE GUTIERREZ

T he quartz is made to resemble marble: thick dove gray veins, their edges blurred, snaking through a background of spilled cream. You look through other samples, small heavy squares excavated from wire shelving, but you return to the first.

I prefer these thicker lines, you say, running your fingertips across the veining. Your husband agrees, and the discussion shifts to the edges and corners of your future kitchen island—straight is more modern, but with a toddler and a baby on the way, perhaps curved is best—and then you hold blue glass subway tile above the countertop, talking about texture and movement. This house you're building: the land is still unmarred, the roots of live oaks tangled beneath hard Texas soil. But you're starting to see it. Imagining it to life, walls conjured around the family you're building, too.

There's something you don't tell your husband about the quartz, though. It's about the veining. How you don't like the thin veins because they are too eerily human, a glimpse into a future of skin sagging like laundry off a line, threaded with brittle blue-veined webs whose work of sweeping blood back toward the heart is almost finished.

The thick veins, though, are like the unexpected glimmer of eels through a stream. They're how you envision the pain running through you. The way it started, its clear origin point where pelvis meets thigh, and eventually spread, snaking up across your pubic bone and down your inner thigh. Pain like bones splintering, or—and this is how you like to imagine it—like a corded tendon, once pink and pliable, hardening slowly until it crystallizes. A hidden piece of you turned suddenly breakable. But also—maybe—stronger.

The first fight after he slipped the pear-shaped diamond onto your finger was at Joshua Tree National Park. A company adventure retreat, significant others invited, sleeping in tents beneath dense constellations of stars. Rock climbing and navigation exercises by day, fireside wine and storytelling by night.

The fight started as your group traipsed, hot and disoriented, across boulders that glow orange in memory. The sun like a heavy hand on your backs, following a guide whose job was less to *guide* than to simply ensure the group's safety throughout the exercise. He sprang over rocks agile as a mountain goat while everyone else grunted and strained, examining a map and compass, glancing behind and squinting ahead at the boulders strewn like giant marbles dropped from an unseen hand. The videographer your company had hired was struggling with her equipment. Here, you said, pass me something. She gave you a grateful smile and two heavy bags, then reached for the hand extended to help her climb onto a higher boulder.

Give them to me, your fiancé said, hands at the straps on your shoulders. His tone sharpened by the heat and the rocks and the pointlessness of the mission.

I've got it, you said, jerking away. Annoyed at how put-out he sounded, offering this help you hadn't asked for, didn't need. People often thought you softer, weaker, than you knew yourself to be. It seemed that he, who should know better, was doing the same. Assuming you couldn't carry the weight you'd knowingly taken on.

And so your voices raised and the embarrassed tears came and it felt as though the cracks in your intimacy were exposed, as though water might seep into them and the two of you, who had recently felt so connected, might break apart into new formations, separate and hard beneath the sun.

* * *

At eleven weeks pregnant, you gripped the horizontal metal poles of a Pilates Cadillac, your feet tucked into fuzzy black straps, your legs splayed into an almost-split. You'd joked, when you first saw this machine, that it looked like a BDSM bed with all its shiny chrome and incomprehensible attachments. Two weeks later, you felt the pain in your groin for the first time. You were on a run, training for an upcoming half marathon. It was one of your stubborn ideas, that you might be able to run thirteen miles while five months pregnant, you and your invisible child whom you would soon see smiling in her 3D ultrasound. Maybe, you thought, remembering the Cadillac, you'd accidentally hurt yourself after all.

Weeks passed. There were tests, bones luminous on dark screens, and tables where men and women with different expertise manipulated the limbs that seemed suddenly to have betrayed you. There was ice and heat, hours lost to fruitless research, message boards and pregnancy forums. There was your husband lifting you from bed, then taking one warm hand to each hip and holding your shifting bones together as you braced against the shatter of your own weight on the ground, and finally there was your sister's old crutch from when she'd fractured her foot and your grandfather's old cane from after his cancer surgeries, both resurrected from your parents' garage over Thanksgiving weekend, and there was no half-marathon and no Pilates and you became a bitter stranger in your own body, the same body in which your invisible child grew, her movements shifting the landscape of your belly, boulders rising, and you feared you might disappear into the pain forever.

* * *

It has a name, but the names of things don't always matter. This is strange for a writer to admit, that the word intended to give a thing meaning is itself meaningless, does not change the thing's essential *thingness*. This is especially true for diagnoses, the names of which often only describe the symptoms.

Your body is not functioning as it should, as it used to, as you had no reason to expect it not to continue? Ah, yes. We call that "dysfunction."

Your pelvic bones feel as though they're coming apart? That's because they are. The pubic symphysis, the cartilaginous joint that connects the left and right superior rami of the pubic bones, has been loosened by the pregnancy hormone relaxin. It's now like a rusty hinge shivering on a doorframe, the door itself wobbly, unable to shut properly, swinging open and banging the wall without warning, denting, becoming dented.

So, yes. You are experiencing a dysfunction of your pubic symphysis. The diagnosis, ergo, is symphysis pubis dysfunction.

The fundamental mystery was not, then, the diagnosis, and perhaps it rarely is, but what would fix it, what would allow you to re-inhabit your own body.

SPD is very common in pregnancy. It usually resolves after delivery.

* * *

You rent stylish maternity clothes from a subscription service. You curl your hair and apply makeup and take weekly bump photos, using an app to compare your invisible baby to fruits you've never tasted: kumquat, rutabaga, durian. You make jokes about your crutch and accept compliments about being "all belly" and brush paint swatches onto the nursery walls.

You nearly scream trying to roll over in bed. You think, Fuck if I'll let this beat me, but it *is* beating you, it's diminishing you each day. You fantasize about pills you can't take, wine you can't drink, anything to *stop feeling.* You wonder if it will really go away. You wonder if you could continue to live with it if it stays. You understand, for the first time, why someone might choose not to.

* * *

The baby is born.

No. That is too passive. You birth your baby, your daughter. You tell the nurses not to touch your legs because you're terrified of being stretched beyond your range of motion, the (maybe) temporary damage becoming permanent. You count the ceiling tiles and stare at the air conditioning vent and feel your husband's hand on your right knee and hear the nurse's voice in your left ear, and you push, and you push, and you push until your lungs are flat, and you suck in another breath, and you push, and you push, and you push, and you scream, feeling as though you are being ripped apart, and for the first time in your life you sob these words: I can't do it!

It seems the work of the pain is done—you have lost the belief in your capacity to endure.

And yet. There is that baby, that dark head slipping past your pubic bone and tucking back in, an endless inch, that head that has already resisted the vacuum, and you wonder what will happen if you truly can't do this, if you truly give up. One more time, the nurse says, fervent in your ear. You can do it, your husband says, and you hear his conviction but also his fear, and you are afraid, too, and so you push, and you push, and you scream, and then finally she is warm and slick on your chest, and you no longer feel any pain.

* * *

Compared to the pregnancy, recovery was easy. You greeted guests at the door with the baby swaddled tight in the crook of your elbow. You grinned, shot through with ecstasy even through the bleeding and cramps and lack of sleep. No crutch! you exclaimed. Everyone asked if the pain was gone, just like that, and no, it wasn't, but what remained was an echo, a shadow, a stain. What remained was possible to bear.

That's how it seemed, anyway, in those first months of learning how to be a mother. But as time passed, the stain darkened in your mind, a haunting. You remembered how stubborn you'd been on those boulders, refusing your soon-to-be husband's help, and how later you'd been strapped into a harness and climbed a seventy-foot rock face, but then, unexpectedly, you'd frozen at the top, unable to bring yourself to turn your back to the void, to trust the rope and the hands that held it. Do you need help? the instructors called from below. You shook your head. I can do it! And, eventually, you did.

You remembered the pregnancy, how completely you came to rely on your husband. How, without resentment or complaint, he'd taken over the shared chores, doing all the cooking, the cleaning, the laundry. He'd supported your weight. He'd held your bones together. He'd kept you from falling completely apart.

You wondered which version of yourself was truer: the brash, able-bodied girl who refused to admit her limitations, or the debilitated woman who had no choice but to accept help, who reached for gratitude but felt mostly defeat. You wondered which version you were now that you were more physically able than during the pregnancy but more timid, more doubtful and afraid, than before. In your body you were like a person whose house has been robbed and who, despite installing an alarm system, never quite feels safe in bed again.

* * *

SPD is statistically likely to return in subsequent pregnancies.

You rolled your eyes when people insisted you'd forget the pain. But your daughter: her wild chestnut curls and wide almond eyes, the same dark amber as the sunburnt leaves at the park by your house. The way she runs with hands waving by her ears and dances to Post Malone in her car seat and exclaims, *Nook!* as she points to birds in the sky and *Oh, no!* as she hurls a toy to the ground. The way she insists it is you, only you, who reads her a story at night, curling into your chest with delicate fingers stroking yours. The vast, impossible love that has broken you open and remade you. The equation is simple, the results the same every time: the pain was worth it.

So, as your daughter grew, you began to think of a sibling playing beside her, the bond that might grow between them, sustaining them later—much later, you hope—after you and your husband are gone.

You began trying. It wasn't easy with your daughter, and you didn't expect it to be easy this time. Spring lengthened into summer and then fall into winter. You were secretly relieved.

Your family signed up for the annual half-marathon, the one for which you'd been training when the pain first began. There were only four weeks until the race, but suddenly it felt important, even necessary, to try training for it. As if there might be some reclamation there, as if soon it might be too late.

You ran a mile that first day, just to see. You'd jogged in uncomfortable fits and starts before, but this was your first full mile in more than two years. The sky was gemstone blue, fences draped in ivy and bougainvillea. You pushed your daughter, now eighteen months old, in the stroller, laughing at your body's boldness, the freedom of the rise and fall.

And so the training began. You ran every other day, with long runs on Sundays. But that first easy mile was a fluke. Your stride was short, legs heavy, jaw clenched. You felt that warning pinch in your groin and envisioned the corded tendon, that thick vein of pink shifting to gray as you ran, mineralizing below the surface of your skin. Sometimes you stopped to walk, but walking hurt more, so you kept running. You paid close attention to your body after each run, ready to stop if the pain lingered or worsened, but it never did.

When the training called for a seven-mile run, you said to your mother, who was also training, This one will tell me if I'm ready. Afterward you hobbled straight-legged, limping, the rest of the afternoon. But you did it.

You said, the following week, The nine-mile run will tell me.

Then, the week before the race, The eleven-mile run will tell me.

And then, the day before the race, you finally signed up. You collected your bib and sensor and went to bed later than you should have and rose before the sun.

It was still dark when you and your parents and brother edged into your corral. You lifted your knees and squatted low to the pavement, shivering in the December chill. You took photos together, grinning and flexing your biceps.

Then you ran. You ran, it felt, toward the pain, as though you were chasing it, daring it, as though you had set a trap and were lying in wait. Within a few miles it was there, your grim companion, and if you slowed down it would win, so you kept pushing forward. You can do it, you hissed to yourself a few times, and you realized that *this* was the reclamation, right here, not the running, not your body, but your belief in your capacity to endure.

Two weeks after the race, you were pregnant.

* * *

You made mood boards for the house you were building, the rooms different each time because the dream was still taking shape. But the quartz countertops with the thick dove gray veining were constant. You designed around them every time.

What would you say if I told you everything that is to come? The virus, the isolation, the overwhelmed hospitals and refrigeration trucks, the death count rising every day? The decision to sell that lot, because when will it be safe to build, and to buy a house instead. The way you carry your daughter through the pain, and carry moving boxes, and carry a baby boy inside you who tumbles through the silent predawn hours—but also how your husband carries you from bed, hands on your hips, and your arms linked around his neck, and how you are grateful, so grateful, to lean your weight against him.

What would you say if I told you to imagine the pain as the molten magma from which quartz is formed? Quartz, hardy and resistant to weathering, the primary component of both mountaintops and sand, its forms and uses boundless, the way it can be eventually ground up and sealed with resin, resulting in something even stronger than when it began. What would you say if I told you the pain is part of that, though not all of it, not by far?

What I mean is: your strength is not simple. It is not binary. It lies neither in stubbornness nor submission, ability nor disability, but in your capacity to endure. To carry the weight when you can and to share it when you can't. One unforeseeable day into the next.

What I'm saying is: You will not disappear this time. You will emerge. You have to.

DAYS OF NEW ORLEANS

GARY SOKOLOW

I know now I can come back and love the leaves like
I once did, their rough underbellies and autumn bleeding,
and I know now how it will balance, the years of fear and
shame, the years of peace to come, how this time I won't cry
passing Mei Mei's Chinese Takeout, the middle-aged man
still alone in the window, his fork tines deep into his sesame
chicken and fried rice, and how this time I will rise from the
pavement, not let the traffic rush over me when she lashes
out at the egg roll and the broccoli, sends me jumping from
a car, how good my feet will feel standing again on Broadway,
and I wonder now how I made it those thousand fluorescent
nights, through tears I thought had run dry, my expiration
into air, and how the vibration of light in New Orleans
would save me, a giant orange abstract in the art museum,
it was part salvation, part hangover, the others back sleeping,
the jittery hotel clerk who warned me off the streets, where
I'd find comfort riding buses, in this city with the dead above
ground, and the living that seemingly was never going to stop.

EVERYTHING IS FINE

JEMIMAH WEI

We sent Grandma out for milk last week and she returned today with a husband. Not just any husband. Her second one, the one we thought died in the war.

Ma and Pa had all but given up hope. They were in grief, stage three: bargaining.

God, let her return safe and healthy, Hanming will give up the drink forever.

God, we ain't ready to lose her, give her back and we'll start tithing again, twenty percent like You commanded.

God, please, just in one piece.

All of that went out the window when she reappeared after lunch. Safe, healthy, happy, and freshly re-betrothed, from the looks of it.

Ma lost her temper immediately. At me. Me!

I told you to go with her, but you're so busy leading your own life, doing god knows what in that room of yours—

In case she falls down, not in case she comes back with a man!

She stormed off to find an extra blanket and wouldn't say another word. Pa followed suit. This always happens. Something big happens in this house and no one will say a thing. We always just continue on, pretending that everything is fine.

Pa used to take me in the Honda on grocery runs, when I was a kid. I'd sit in the backseat and watch, terrified, as he drove with his hand in Aunty Lucy's lap. After each trip to the store, the Honda would smell like expired Anna Sui for days. When we next got in the car to go to church, I'd stare at Ma, waiting for her to notice. But she'd just slide the Sunday cassette into the stereo, filling the car with hymns like Amazing Grace or O Come All Ye Faithful.

Then Aunty Lucy got too big for her britches. She left a crumpled tissue behind, carefully wedged into the passenger seat, stained with bright red lipstick. That Sunday, I almost exploded with excitement as Ma slowly pulled it out from under the cushions of her seat, dangling it between her thumb and forefinger. Pa's face went white, I think he almost had a heart attack. I couldn't see all of Ma's expression from the backseat, and strained against my seatbelt trying not to be too obvious, but all she did was wind the window down and toss the tissue out. Then, it was Amazing Grace all over again.

I was loyal to Ma back then. I cornered her in the kitchen and told her I'd take her side in the divorce proceedings, no problem. The courts were likely to grant her full custody, on account of her being a woman and all. She didn't even miss a beat, just told me to go make my bed.

Pa got mad at Aunty Lucy for her antics, and I never saw her again. I ignored him out of principle for about a month, but I don't think he realized.

The only sane person in this house is Grandpa #4. I went to check in on him, see how he was doing, given the recent turn of events. He is the whole reason we always need milk. Everything he eats has to be mushed up in it, or he won't swallow. But he didn't seem to realize that his wife had traipsed off with another man.

C'mon, Grandpa, I whispered to him, fight. This ain't right.

He gurgled in laughter. A little bit of drool escaped from his lip, dribbling down his chin. No one was looking, so I wiped it off with the bottom of his singlet and took the chance to put my face to his scalp. He smells real good all the time now, like baby powder and milk. When I get out of this house and go to college, I swear, that's all I'm gonna do, try and invent a cologne that smells just like that. I can't imagine anyone who wouldn't be into it. Except Grandma, apparently.

Back in the living room, Grandma and the newly resurrected Grandpa #2 were sitting on our couch, cooing and watching TV. I guess I get it, it's not like they broke up back in the day. She thought he'd died. Someone dies in the war, they're a martyr. And then when you bump into them at the bodega after fourteen years, it's a miracle. So yeah, I'm not dumb, I get it.

Still. Call me old fashioned, but she's a married woman. And what are we going to do now with our surplus of grandpas? The image of Grandma, squished between Grandpa #2 and #4 in her little cot, made me shudder.

Grandma, I hissed.

She continued watching TV. She's a bit deaf. I raised my voice. Grandma.

Before I could deliver my lecture on adultery, Ma came charging out of the storeroom, cleaning materials in hand. She didn't even look at her two-timing mother-in-law. Go, she said. We need milk.

She was really furious. I chewed on my indignation all the way to the bodega. Nobody takes me seriously in this house. Just because I'm the youngest. Doesn't mean I don't have the right to an opinion. They were out of all the good milk, the Organic Valleys and Meijis and Dairylands. I thought about just getting a carton of the store brand milk, but the last time we got that, Grandpa #4 spent a week farting miserably in his room. The poor guy. He looked so hopeful that each fart would be his last, but less than half an hour would pass before he let rip again. It really broke my heart.

I got the Ronnybrook. It's normally not something we'd even consider, because of how expensive it is, but I figured Grandpa #4 could really use a break. Ma could yell at me later. I brought it to the counter. Tanuj raised an eyebrow while ringing it up.

You all good, buddy?

What else could I say? I just nodded, thinking of Ma. *Everything is fine.*

THE BUMP

BRITTANY TERWILLIGER

I know Scottie is a little shit and when he cajoles my dad to let him take the 4-wheeler out I scream a little inside because I know he's going to do something stupid, but my dad lets him go anyway, probably thinking it's better to just let him break a wrist or an ankle and learn his lesson, except he doesn't learn his lesson, he comes back twenty minutes later saying he's not sure but he thinks maybe he hit something, says it looked like a mongoose, which makes my dad snort and reply "you didn't hit a mongoose," but Scottie swears that's what it was and asks us to go check, so my dad and I head for his truck and Scottie says he doesn't want to go, which is typical Scottie, so we go without him, idling slowly toward the spot he described, windows down, cold air biting our foreheads, until we see it, a red fox, lying in the middle of the road, not dead, every few seconds lifting its head to look around, unable to move its body, and it has the sweetest, most soulful eyes, like it knows us, and my chin starts to tremble, and my dad says "oh my god," and I say "Dad we can't just leave it here," and he says "I can put it out of its misery," and tells me he'll leave it up to me, and I imagine how scary we must look from down there, this big growling machine approaching his defenseless, paralyzed little body, and I hate Scottie so much, back playing video games in our warm house because he's too fragile for this, and I look at my dad, both of us huffing tears, and say "do it," and the bump-bump never leaves my body.

GRANDMOTHER IN SILHOUETTE

G.H. MOSSON

Do you recall your grandmother in an image
more seared and aflame than any desk-kept photograph,
in an image that flashes, blinds, and trembles—
which recalls you, making you
that age again, and tickled
by those stories and stuffed
with her cooking again?
It's a human candle that will burn
the spice and backstory of her laughter
as you excavate your own,
elbow deep in darkness.

ROSE AS IN ROSA

ANTHONY AGUARO

As in the elegant woman,
menthol cigarillo in hand,
puff-puff-puffing,
sitting nearest to the back—
door. History is a door many,
many have walked through.
There was a garden that,
too, smelled of Lavandula
bathed in amber-light.
History has a way of, too,
being illuminated on:
sifted through, like a
rosarium pretty in its
variation. Rosa, as in
rose, is at the bud of
the cigarette. History, too,
has a way of many
endings. Rosa dancing
in a red dress. The floor
beneath her, erased,
leaving wet soil. The roof
above her, flooded into.
A thousand roses
sprouting on her red

dress and she just sings
Lo Mucho Que Te Quiero.
History, then, too, has
snuck its way into song:
something sung to Rosa.
The roses in the garden
looking like wisps of
       carmine smoke.

ST. JOHN'S ROAD

DONALD BERGER

A small boar turf war, a small bee playing with the bottom of the table,
some really small wind, and forty, fifty stages of green.
O I'll be back as soon as I get that pancake, the spicey one with kim chi
in it,
the thing that makes you feel.

Dave sticks his car's nose into the driveway,
Fresh on the Move in truck form pulls around,
shade right with almost two people out.
Religiously I swing
the club through I think a boy's voice
over the water.

You don't want to overwater
and could hear the bird swerve
before the walker said "in a little while."
Have that mentality where almost no leaves,
the click on a dog's leash move
the baby swinging off the side of the father's chest.
The bicycle sounding like a cricket.

Tomorrow there might be nothing
to say except Move your car a little further away from the tree.
Try again.

I watch somebody steal
a parking spot, it's true, facing the wrong way,
while birds congregate without crossing the border.

I've had the most unbelievable time
and am afraid of the direction he's walking in,
Just write sentences, the rabbits tell me,
while the brain cues up,
the motor of something relaxing shuts,
starts up again, at the reflection of the blue button.

The forest was close
and young.
The rooster's horrible.
Pat's car sounds like a truck.

This is normalcy's flavor.
"Say my phone dies
in the middle of the road ... "

I love how nothing
worries, how not eating
doesn't faze, how a green shirt
suits, peppermint.

The poems (don't) take too long to read.
Whatever that bee's thinking, I'm thinking too.
I'll be on the porch, fairest listening,
I'll be on the porch for all of it.

TRICK SHOT

DAVIS MACMILLAN

H e has a nice touch. This is the thing that he thinks at night, when he worries that he doesn't have anything at all, that he's completely and colossally missed his shot, which he never really had in the first place since he was never good enough.

He has nice touch. That is something Billy knows about himself. He thinks something and the ball does it. Not everyone can do that.

It's also what keeps him employed. Until recently, he coached kids Monday, Wednesday, and Friday at the Tommy Jackson Soccer Clinic ('Real Football' and Atlas leaping up to head the world on the official shirt). This involved running 9-, 10-, and 13-year-olds through cones, passing drills, shooting drills. He'd get down on his knees and correct their form, one hand on the thigh and one hand on the calf. He'd yell at them to keep their heads up as they dribble. He'd yell at them to stay on their toes.

That's on pause now, along with everything else. With the rest of his time Billy makes trick videos: rainbows, flicks, take-ons, shots. He's trying to build a following.

An example: the video opens with him facing three defenders (friends he recruited to stand in a line and look menacing). He flicks the ball over each of their heads in quick, rhythmic unison then kicks the ball into the goal. Another example, he kicks a ball forty feet through a basketball hoop. These got 8,000 and 15,000 views, respectively.

The economics of the trick shot YouTube video are challenging. That's how Billy explains it to anyone who asks. "My best video has more than

20,000 views but YouTube doesn't start paying until you have a bunch of videos like that. Really a bunch of videos with more views more than that." People generally nod and tell him to keep at it.

The pandemic hasn't made things easier. He's made do so far with videos shot in his apartment. For example, he juggled a roll of toilet paper, bouncing it end over end between his feet and knees and chest and head until it began to unravel. By the end of the video the paper had unfurled in a ghostly strand through his bedroom. It looked like someone was playing a prank on him. That one got about 10,000 views.

He's running out of ideas. This is what leads him to the roof. He knew about the building thanks to a friend who, the year before, had invited him to a rooftop happy hour that needed more guests (the details were never made clear, all he was told was that it had to seem like a good party for the vodka brand or skateboarder in attendance). That day, he'd pushed open the heavy rooftop door to find himself in a mock tiki bar populated exclusively by 20-somethings in Brooks Brothers shirts.

Mid-pandemic, security is lax. It just takes a bit of confidence, a quick walk past the front desk, and he's in the stairwell. Forty flights later and he's on the roof.

There, the reality of the plan hits him. For some reason, the surface of the roof is no longer blank concrete. Instead, someone has covered it in tiny white pebbles. It's as if the building needed a bit of extra weight on top to keep it sunk into the ground. It's as if someone was worried that the roof would fly off. The pebbles make it hard to walk confidently. The pebbles make it more likely that he'll slip.

Still, he sets up. He spends a few minutes scoping out shots with his phone. The goal is to maximize the amount of sky and buildings. The goal is to make the audience feel like he's floating in the air.

Then he's ready. The video doesn't require much, comparatively speaking. All he's got to do is juggle. He'll kick the ball higher and higher, and control it each time. He wants his audience to feel like he's kicked the ball into space and then caught it. He might add some flames when he edits.

Things go fine, mostly. Early on he kicks a pebble and watches it roll off the edge of the building. He thinks, briefly, about its trajectory on the way down and the time until it reaches terminal velocity. He tries not to think about what's below.

The juggling begins. The ball spins up off his foot and onto his knee, off his knee and onto his head. Then it drops down and he fires it straight up into the air and out of frame. He watches it back down, catches it, controls it once (think of Ronaldinho and the crossbar) then fires it back into the air. He does this three times before he loses it.

Maybe his weight was wrong. Maybe his feet were pointing the wrong direction. For whatever reason, the ball flies off his foot at an angle, back over his head, just narrowly missing his nose. He turns and watches it, the white of the pleather glinting in the sun. For a few seconds it looks like it might fly forever, it's parabola cut off halfway so that it continues to sail ever upward until it hits the sun. Then, imperceptibly at first, it starts to bank back towards earth. He thinks of rockets. He thinks of how much trouble he's going to be in.

Perhaps the whole time his problem has been one of instincts. Certainly now he should be running away. That would be the move of someone who'd correctly assessed the situation. He doesn't do that. Instead he stands on the roof, phone now in hand, filming the projectile he launched as it flies towards the Earth.

SING AWAY, MY SISTER

CATE MCGOWAN

This song of X-rays, coming from a chorus of millions of black holes, fills the entire sky.
—NASA's Jet Propulsion Laboratory, "Chorus of Black Holes Sings in X-Rays," 28 July 2016

Where does all the light go? Sister, is it sucked like matter into supermassive black holes,
pulled through eclipses & star fields to a doom

of darkness, a place where nothing escapes except X-ray music? The more
a black hole takes, the more it wants.

My sister, you ask, what do I know of robberies & cruelty? Oh, I know.
Planets, nebulae, far-flung quasars.

Crystal, silver, china, gold. Gone. Sister, you blew open the family safe.
You sang as you stole. Your soprano

sucked the energy from rooms, keened away with off-key phrases,
while I, the quiet alto on the front row,

mouthed harmonies, vibratoed my white dwarf warbles. I sit
on my back stoop & seethe about you,

2020

admiring glamorous constellations where bodies orbit
whorling cores. A trick of the light.

The moon wanes, & a nightingale calls through a copse
at the pond's edge. At a space-age

distance, I clock the universe's massacres, its dark
soffits, underhanded sky. Brutality's

acceptable, even beautiful in the residue
of aftermaths, of orifices

dark, obsidian. Those chasms wrangle
yellow dwarves, red giants,

swallow fire after fire, snuff luminescence,
until all event-horizon evidence

disappears, the picked-off galaxies gobbled
whole through mine shafts.

The world sings aubades about density,
brags about building mass.

Apologies arrive too late now, vowels
on top of vowels, your

wavelength on a loop. Your serenades
burst energy as they

burgle, such raucous choruses only
observed/heard through

astronomers' special telescopes.
We lose so much to greed.

Sister, what a shame these naked
ears of ours, such weak

instruments, aren't alerted
to this universe's

rowdy record of carnage,
its score of astral

flashes, clicks & groans,
aural paisleys

airborne. Black-hole
bitch, stop

your whining. Sister,
stop your

high, low frequencies,
your X-ray

croons vespering,
speeding

away through
night.

Stop.

ONCE I WAS AN ANIMAL (AFTER MARY OLIVER)

MEGAN PILLOW

There's a woodpecker perched on the side of the house outside my bedroom window. He spends his days drumming against the wood, flying away, coming back to drum again. Maybe he's nesting, searching for food. Maybe he's just drumming out his desires for a mate. I don't know why he does it. But every time I hear him, I want to tell him to consider the cedar, the maple, the sycamore at the edge of the porch, anything but the dead wood of the house. Every time I hear the drumming, I think *it's me, it's me.*

Once I was an animal. Not a bird or a bat, not the soft-bodied kind, but an animal, slick-bodied, all heat and teeth and nails. I used to fuck and scream and gorge myself. I used to run my tongue along a slab of skin and decide whether or not to eat it.

I am not an animal anymore.

I am rooted in a room, rooted in a bed that I once shared with someone. The walls are thick as bark around me. Outside, the moon, the trees, the silver drift of snow.

The year is a spell, and I am casting about inside it.

There is no one here to touch me, so I touch myself. I think of the way I lick my lips before I kiss someone, of the way I lean in, of the shock of their skin against mine. I think of sliding three fingers between the breasts of someone in a club somewhere, of wiping that trickle of sweat away, of putting my fingers in my mouth to taste it. I think of the way someone will pull me to the edge of the bed and then turn me over, of the way they will run their hand down every knob of my spine while I pant and beg for it, of the way they will grip my hips and then thrust themselves inside. I think of the way a person says my name when they are inside of me, of the way they say my name when my fingers are inside of them, and I come, and I come, and I come, but there is no real place to come to.

There is no one here to touch me, so I dream of touch instead. Last night, I dreamed that someone took a fingertip and wrote the word *love* across my chest and cracked it open, but everything inside had gone to seed.

The year is a spell, and here we are, one lone letter from the end of it. Here we are, at the end, and yet I know that once a spell is cast, there must be something to break it, or it will cast on and on and on.

Somewhere beyond this room, beyond this midnight alone in the middle of cuffing season, there will be something more than just imagining. There will be music, the sound of the sun, the lift of geese into a clear blue sky behind the halo of a lover's hair. There will be a crush of people that is safe again.

Someday, beyond this midnight, I will make love again, and perhaps the person will keep it.

I do not believe that that someday is soon.

For now, I root down in my bed, and I think of you. You think of me too. Here I am, the imagining, moving across the fields and forests, across the ice floes that thread the rivers, here I am on your doorstep. I am taking you in my arms. I am kissing you. We burrow into your bed together, skin to skin, and I say to you: someday, we will be animals again.

Meanwhile, the world goes on.

2021

THE LAST TIME I CRIED WAS IN 2015

KRYS MALCOLM BELC

O ur third was a baby: fat, baldheaded, toothless. I don't remember much from then but I'm certain I cried when he would not sleep and I wanted to. In his crib, in the little now-illegal sleeper, in our bed he would not sleep at all while my partner worked the night shift. I knelt beside his crib and held a pacifier in his mouth and I cried. When asked in a job interview in 2019 why I thought I was resilient enough to work as an educator in a pediatric oncology clinic, I waited a long time, too long I worried, before I said, *Because I am transgender.* I looked away from my interviewer's face, out the hospital windows onto construction eating West Philadelphia. I left the hospital through huge sliding doors and I bought myself a donut. Everyone is right, the world is ending in too many ways. The places that defined my life before this past year—my children's schools and patients' schools—they've changed, shuttered or soured or both. Our third is now almost five and he has curly hair and many nicknames and he cries all the time. Our family has been almost nowhere in months. One day our third son had a preschool class, a life, and the next day it was gone. I look at him crying and I feel deeply worried. About his future. About anyone's. I got the job. In my work I hear stories, about all the things that can happen to a child's body, about the ways schools, these places I love so deeply, how they do not see bodies on the margin. I hear so many stories, they pile up on each other but still I do not cry. Wanting to does not make it happen. My email headings: *Re: My patient/*

2021

Your student _____ . My emails: *I can't imagine planning for this school year; can we connect to talk about* _____ *?* I call the school nurse the school counselor the teacher and I say, *I will work with his oncologist to get you a treatment summary* and I say *Chemotherapy can affect learning long-term, not just during treatment* and I wonder, do I feel so little because I must to keep going, do I feel so little because I am resilient, or do I feel so little because I take testosterone? Nearly five years of these shots, no tears. What are we supposed to feel? We call the child psychologist because our third will not stop lying on the floor crying. He says he has more sad feelings than most people. My partner and I trade peer-reviewed research on early childhood depression and we pay the psychologist whatever she wants. By our estimation the feelings one has in childhood may persist forever, one's whole life. That loneliness, my loneliness. One day he had his little life and the next, gone. Maybe I am not resilient. Maybe testosterone has just stopped me from crying. Simple. I miss the glittering windows of the hospital, but for now I make my phone calls and send my emails from a child's bedroom slash office in the same house where I last cried. When our third was a baby. I remember his bald head cupped in my hands, pacifier pressed gently into his soft lips, and I stand at the bedroom window looking out onto our ending world.

AS A PERSON OF SINGLE EXPERIENCE

CHRISTOPHER GONZALEZ

When asked in high school, say the problem is you're too nice, everyone says you're way too nice. Chalk it up to the Friendzone, Nice Guys Finish Last. Or any other bullshit ideas about sex and dating presented to teenage boys, adopted and unchallenged by you and your friends. You're not some radicalized incel, thank god, but yikes—the same toxic seed was planted, who cares that it didn't fully grow? Don't think about what you believed then without a side-eye and the red burn of embarrassment.

When asked in college, say something about not being fit enough, white enough, rich enough, or, hell, interesting. What do you have to offer anyone? Keep your heart clenched between a fist with one knuckle raised until someone trusts you enough with hers. When she does: fumble, drop it. This isn't a command, but a summary.

When asked again in your early twenties, say it's not written in the stars. Maybe not everyone is meant to find this specific kind of happiness, the one built out of companionship and shared experience, and maybe you have to be OK with that. Even now you can see yourself waking up in ten years, nearing forty, and finding not much has changed. The fear won't be that no one will pick you, it's that you'll be unable to open up, to trust, to build and grow and try and dare. You, forever in the way.

Try speed dating. Once. It's literary themed, which is insufferable but something you can work with. You like books. Unfortunately, it's heteronormative—M/F pairings only.

Everyone has to pick a pseudonym from a book. Settle on the name Yunior, because Junot Díaz is your favorite author at the time. Understand now that this was probably a huge red flag to 10/11 of your dates. Yunior, the womanizer, the cheater. Yunior, the stand-in for Díaz himself, the abuser. It was important to mark yourself as Latino, so you went with what felt like the only choice from your limited reading, a pool of books in which you saw no queer and fat Boricua men. Spend six minutes each with a Jane, an Emma, an Elizabeth, a Hermione, a Jo. Meet an Ifemelu and talk about how much you both love the color yellow until time runs out. Wonder how one complimentary beer was supposed to get you through this.

When you receive your two matches, email both and ask them out for drinks. One will respond, tell you she's sick but would love to meet up in a week. Offer a date and a time; when you don't hear back, accept that it's fine not to follow up.

Love is love is love is love. But fuck it, have sex. Download the apps.

Meet men in hotels, in their apartments; invite a select few to yours. You're out to friends, but hooking up feels like a separate life, one that exists only in the dark. After the first few there's nothing of note to tell anyone. None of them lead to anything more.

There is a man, however, twenty years your senior, who invites you over during the day, lets you experiment with topping. Enjoy the taste of cigarettes on his tongue, the calluses on his hands when his thumb slips into your mouth. Trust him enough to try bottoming—he won't say anything when you bleed, but he'll quickly retrieve paper towels. He'll let you clean up in the bathroom and won't make a big deal when you leave, panicked. Later, months later, he'll pick you up one night and drive you back to his place. Along the highway, he'll slide a hand up your shorts and you'll nibble on his ear. Fuck him hard in his bed, then run away at 2AM. Grab a decaf iced coffee from the 24-hour Dunkin outside of the subway stop. Not until you're on the train should you question why you always flee.

To say you grew up with a healthy relationship model would be a lie. Your parents are divorced, which is for the best, and you watched your mom date disappointing man after disappointing man until she met you stepfather. By then, you were too jaded. All you can think about is how awful men can be: liars and cheaters and emotionally stunted ghouls, taking in the love of a woman and offering nothing in return. You witnessed your father yell at women, his anger so easily accessible, the snap of a twig. And though you didn't witness it, you heard about him throwing a bottle at an ex-girlfriend's head when he discovered she was cheating. I'd tell you not to think about these things, but the stories are there inside of you, festering for years, all pus and mold.

Watch your friends slide into relationships. Watch them move in with their significant others and turn apartments into homes. There is a year where you attend the wedding of three couples, six friends. Dress up and drink and dance and celebrate because you are happy for their happiness. At the end of each party, take a Lyft home with your best friend, both of you drunk off your asses. Talk about your favorite parts of the weddings. Talk about the future you imagined for yourself but which feels less and less like a possibility. Cry, but tell yourself as long as the tears are gone when you get out of the car, they don't count.

Remember the friends you no longer see. The ones you'd catch up with every six months after graduating from college. Grabbing drinks in dark bars, going for long, meandering walks hours after the sun had set. You'd ask how they were doing, how was everything at work, how was their partner, were things still good? And in turn, they'd ask you if you were seeing anyone, have you met anyone, are you dating, are you on the apps, it's been so long. That question, once upon a time, could deflate you like a balloon, drown the room in so much air you'd wonder if you might blow away. The answer, always: I'm not. Depending on the friend, they might change the subject quickly, bring it back to someone else from school, an update on another insignificant life. Some friends frown. Some friends let the silence roll on. Look back. What hurt more? To be asked if you had tried to love again, or to not be asked at all?

TO BE OR NOT TO BOP (FOR DIZZY GILLESPIE)

ROBERT FELDMAN

rider leapfroggin over Union Square El
atop bent trumpet
fresh from decimatin the competition,
this angel rainin visions
strolls in from Philadelphia packin a struggle rhythm,
blowin by the skins in lightnin 64th notes
pickpocketin the soaked drummer,
destroyin February midnight Broadway's dashed lines,
headin north up the FDR
uptempo music forever movin
exaggeratin into the air of possibilities—
to be or not to bop,
absolutely no question

hushed snow fallin
white poppy round midnight winterwashed Harlem,
Dizzy never goin back,
he and Bird realizin long ago
the first time's always perfect, man,
brother deuces trumpetin and blowin down the East River,
annihilatin the gates clean off 52nd St,

mad fickle lovers removin dark glasses
decipherin naked notes—
composin one more Mr. Jones, their generational copilot

and when Max and Monk's uptempo drives them further,
14 melodies at once
burst out Dizzy's parachuted cheeks
mergin into one silverthroated voice,
flatted fifths soar
speakin in whispers
the exact Minton's of harmony,
and those uptown streets
and those bedsheets go
rollin way back downtown,
to a place where unclothed cognac sunset waves
run crashin off Rockaway Beaches,
to a place where this giant heart lives on
touched by his child's artistry,
livin on laughin and blowin,
forever dinin out on the Blues

REAPPROPRIATION SONNET

REBECCA BORNSTEIN

"Steal from work! Because work is stealing from you!"—CrimethInc

At twenty-three, in the deli whites of the grocery store
covered in chicken blood and viscera until midnight,
I wasn't thinking about stealing. It was more
that I was hungry and the food was right

in front of me, waiting for the compost in the chlorine-
studded dishpit. I ate the piece of pizza with a kid-sized bite
taken out of the crust end. I scooped up the oily greens
left at the bottom of the stew pot. My bosses told us to sit tight

and wait for a raise that wasn't coming. Instead, we found a way
to feed ourselves by taking what they couldn't sell
and sneaking it out in take-out boxes—grey

potatoes, fried chicken hardened to a wooden shell.
We ate until we were full and rolled the garbage to the dumpster's bay
a little lighter, knowing only we could tell.

MC HAMMER RALLIES

SUZANNE S. RANCOURT

Heel strikes burst between flip flops' unequal slaps
they are ADP mini explosions in humanity's concourse
terminal air in a can. Radio squelch reverberates
amongst anxious passengers—fills in the gaps
around ear buds—heads bob

Airport audio systems transport me back to my first transistor radio
Mum bought from Sears & Roebuck for each of us kids
sporting faux leather cases that bright Bakelite red, turquoise
or flaming orange leaked out like the ear phone strung from a 3.5 jack
Man, we was cool and my orange transistor went everywhere—a
phenomenon

Storms rally in Kentucky and grow pendulous with black clouds
Sundown Towns and delayed flights. Somewhere, a seal is broken
MC Hammer leaks out from under a nodding head: you can't touch this

CATS AS CLASSIC
NEW ENGLAND DIRTBAGS

BLAKE Z. RONG

I n the summer he takes him to the creek to show him a dead body. They follow the leaning fences through the mud and the leeches and the pesky poisoned rhododendron; they balance on fallen moss-covered logs one paw before the other, feeling a thrill akin to Indiana Jones across the low and muddy water, stagnant between the greyish brown rocks. Moose picks a leech from his front paw with his teeth. Marshmallow bats at a yellowing fern and the ladybug dangling from a single spiral. He eats the ladybug with a flick of his sandpapery tongue. The body is a raccoon's, a few days old with its guts all fileted under the July sun; they sense the toxic warning with their thin pink noses. Plus, it's not even in a creek but on the road: Boylston Street to Prospect Street to Old Mill Road and towards the quarry where it meets Route 128. They circle the corpse gingerly—tails lowered, as if in respect, the downward arch of anxiety. Marshmallow's tail is a dustbroom black and majestic, with its fur as wide as a baseball bat. Moose's tail is slender and tapering like a German sausage, black but with speckled hairs of white, the hair of a respected news anchor who occasionally lies.

Moose sniffs at the splayed-out raccoon and Marshmallow calls him a chickenshit and dares him to actually touch it.

Fuck you, Moose says, *you touch it.*

Don't speak to your brother like that, says Marshmallow, *I'm older than you. Show some respect.*

Oh yeah? Well, I dare you to lick it.

Dare you to pick it up and carry it all the way home in your mouth.

No way. I double dog dare you to, uh, hump it.

You're such a dumbass. You can't do double dog dares already, dumbass.

They know to head back before dinnertime. Some of the neighborhood bullies pass by on BMX bikes and flip them off, but they ignore them. It is still light out, pink and blue. The pavement is warm. They steal some plywood from the tract houses under construction behind their street and build bike ramps in the garage. Moose half-heartedly saws at a few pieces into triangles but Marshmallow does most of the work. Later that night a water gun fight breaks out—all the kittens in the neighborhood come out with their Super Soakers, high-pressure artillery that could bombard the Normandy coast. The two tabby sisters Lizzy and Cici corner Moose behind their backyard shed and lay waste to his fur at point-blank range. Annoyed, Moose spends the rest of the night licking himself clean while Marshmallow fires up Goldeneye on the N64. Temple, Klobbs, first to 5 kills. Moose watches his older brother destroy his enemies with a look across his face like some kind of awe. It is still warm out.

* * *

Every day in the fall, Marshmallow rolls a joint and watches the DVD commentary of *The Boondock Saints* while splayed out on a torn leatherette couch that is somehow always warm. On one random Tuesday afternoon, while half-drunk himself, he presents Moose with his first alcoholic drink: a lukewarm glass bottle of Mike's Hard Lemonade that he pilfered from their neighbor's deck. Moose can sense every whisker tingling. I can't feel my lips! he yells, and Marshmallow laughs and laughs and laughs until he starts coughing, hacking up a hairball the size of a Vienna sausage that lands with a plop onto the wet and sticky Olefin carpet.

I want some tater tots, says Moose. *Put 'em in the oven. Four-fifty. Crisp 'em up nice.*

We're all out, Marshmallow says, bitterly, as if it's Moose's fault. *Freezer's empty. Plus I keep asking you to clean out that nasty-ass toaster oven.*

Can we go to Wendy's? I'll be your guardian or adult or whatever.

Marshmallow laughed. *Yeah right. You'll never fucking be an adult.*

After some more convincing Marshmallow—dogeared learners permit in tow—drives them to the Wendy's in Edgemere in a rusty Mazda 323 hatchback that he had traded $200 in pot for. Moose crawls across the dashboard. They blast Godsmack and Dropkick Murphys as they speed on the thickly settled streets, not quite winding roads and not quite suburbia, past old women angrily gesturing at them to slow down. Fuck you, Marshmallow yells out the window, I am slow! The Mazda nearly stalls in the drive-thru. On the way back Moose watches Marshmallow put away four Spicy Chicken Sandwiches with one paw on the steering wheel and it is the most impressive thing he has ever seen in his life.

Winter howls through the trees like an injured wolf. Marshmallow grows out his wild and unruly mane, spends the next few months wearing the same stained 107.3 WAAF hoodie with holes in the sleeves for his thumbs, black cargo shorts from Spag's on Route 9, stops licking himself just to see if he can get away with it. On the mornings at ten degrees Fahrenheit he drives past the bus stop and yells at the middle schoolers: cold enough for you, you pussies? As if it's their fault for reacting to the wind chill. His voice all gravely and forceful as if trying on a costume, acting a role for which he never should have been cast.

All winter long it's plastic sleds flung into the deep-packed forests, icy snowballs with rocks in the center, frozen pellets in the hopper of a Tippman 98, the paintballs ricocheting like musket fire. That long winter Moose stays indoors, burying his face into soldering irons and wiring diagrams. He sniffs at the heady smoke coiling from plastic and tin, installs stereo equipment in his brother's Mazda: twin Sony Xplōd subs in the trunk, 800-watt Kicker amps, a Kenwood DVD player in the dash that Marshmallow just happened to find one day—all custom wooden enclosures, sprayed with flocking to look like it came from the factory. He hears his brother punching holes through the drywall. He could always use some more electrical equipment.

One afternoon Marshmallow comes down the basement stairs with his friend Brisket, shy and shaggy-haired. So yeah, he says to Brisket, this is my brother, what a fuckin' nerd.

Aw man he can't be that bad.

* * *

You finish that computer yet Moose?

Yeah like ages ago. You saw it, it's in my room. But I'm never gonna let you in my room.

Oh I've been there. I've stolen all your beer that you hide under your bed. I know where you hide your porno.

Shut up! I don't have any porn!

I hide my pornography in my dad's coffee table. Right where the old remotes go. It's the last place he'll ever look.

Nobody cares, Brisket. I'm here making fun of my stupid brother for jacking off in this basement all day.

Dude I'm doing all this for you! Wiring all of these harnesses for your shitbox car. Can you stop being a dick to me for once in your life?

Brisket stares at the two, not knowing what to say, and decides to curl up on the stairs and lick his butthole.

Marshmallow glares at Moose. This will be something Moose remembers for years: that sensation of being in the basement with nowhere to go the only exit blocked and you are about to claw your way out of your own fur.

Marshmallow's longer hair allows him to hide deep into his hoodie, where he keeps his Sony Discman, his nascent inner monologue drowned out by Tool and System of a Down and Limp Bizkit's seminal *Chocolate Starfish and the Hot Dog Flavored Water.* The winter turns to grey sludge the consistency of concrete, squishy and gravely between his toe beans, Moose—trying to eviscerate the sensation of cold from his petite bony structure, trying to suffer for his bushido code, he must suck it up, must control his shivering until it is imperceptible underneath his Goodwill Army surplus jacket, where the roundness of his backside rises up and down and nobody can see it unless they bury your face in his soft and scratchy domestic short hair, to hear his purring like a dull, low humming.

***

When the spring arrives, Marshmallow takes Lizzy to senior prom. *I thought you said prom was lame,* said Moose.

No way, he says. *She's in heat bro.*

He's too tough to admit that he's had a crush on her since 8th grade. He's afraid to tell his brother how his breath slows down when she walks down the stairs to the cafeteria for square pizza and tater tots, and for a moment he stops grinning at freshmen to get in line and stand close behind her and breathe deep. He doesn't know that Brisket, Stella, Doctor Mario, Bernard J. Katz Attorney At Paw, and the foreign exchange student Chairman Meow have all gotten to her first. Moose is fixed and therefore has no energy left. In the bathroom Marshmallow runs his lines over and over, all of his best rehearsed jokes, recycled bits from Dane Cook albums. After an eternity he emerges in his rented tuxedo, his clip-on bowtie all askew; Moose notices that his fly is down but doesn't bother telling him.

How's my hair?

Gross. Greasy as hell.

Excellent.

***

The summer before Marshmallow goes off to college he calls himself Captain Marshmallow—a dignified role, an occupation, as if in command of a sailing ship or a battalion. Moose starts to wear a black cowboy hat, cocked to one ear and constantly falling off. It makes him look like a villain which is exactly what he wants. He chews on the straps until they fall off and then he bats them around until they roll underneath the auditorium bleachers.

At Amherst, Captain Marshmallow develops a crush on his English Comp teacher. Daphne is young and long-haired with bright yellow eyes and she likes to lie down where the sunbeam goes, her tortoiseshell colors aglow as she follows the light. She just married a good boy named Hank whose fur is entirely black except a triangular patch on his belly, so white it seems trimmed like a well-groomed ski trail. There is a dignity in the way they sit. They perch atop dumpsters, statuesque, smoking Maverick menthols, glaring at the passing cars. They push their butts off the dumpster lid. He smells like fresh printer paper and warmth. She smells like cherry stems and radiator heat. She licks at his flank with her tongue and feels a low frequency, rising on the last note in patterns of four, and repeating, like radio signals from Siberia. After Lizzy broke his plum-sized heart it is everything that Captain Marshmallow wants in his life.

That first semester Captain Marshmallow falls in with a clowder of libertines who drop shrooms in state park reservoirs, who throw plastic spoons at midnight screenings in black-box theaters, who resemble patchwork broken Furbies in body and spirit. He stands on tables, raising his haunches, shouting in defiance in unison in protest against things he hasn't yet learned. He listens to Fleet Foxes and Joy Division and Kings of Leon before anyone knew who they were. Music he used to make fun of. He kisses a calico named Princess Dumptruck as well as an orange boy named Willie Nelson—at first on a bet, and then, one more time when nobody's looking.

At the Union Station bus terminal Moose picks him up in the Mazda. It is a crisp fall day and the air smells like pine needles and diesel. Captain Marshmallow tries to make conversation, tells Moose he's gonna become a writer someday. He reads Moose a poem he wrote about "the attainment of possibility." Moose rolls his eyes—first at the poem and then at the banality of this small talk: he's already said that he's gonna apply to WPI for electrical engineering, swear to God, but he failed AP Calculus this semester, and last week Cici turned him down to go see 2Fast 2Furious, so what's the point of anything anymore? *Later me and Brisket and Doctor Mario are gonna hit up Sonic and then get hammered at the quarry*, Moose tells his brother. *Then adds, you're welcome to join.*

On his custom-built computer Moose plays Counterstrike, screaming curse words into the microphone. He watches gory Flash videos on Newgrounds. He stays in his room all day. Yowling at all hours of the night, he pisses under the bed and on top of the sheets, scrawls nonsensical phrases up and down his arm in a fat red Sharpie. He claims that he's inventing a new language, the words inescapable. Now his brother sneers at him for what he's become, he says—as if one semester at Amherst can undo what you fundamentally are? Fuck off.

At night Moose goes for a drive in the Mazda. Boylston Street to Prospect Street to Old Mill Road. Cracks on the dashboard point the way north. Through dense rows of corn off the side of the two-lane highway, still green in their stalks, all chaos and stringy when viewed up close. Past the rows of triple-deckers, past the white-steepled churches, into thickets of eastern hemlocks, Holden, West Boylston, Princeton, Wachusett Mountain, moving in slow motion, almost dragged backwards, doomed to repeat the same asphalt squiggles in an infinite loop.

When he was still a kitten, he had figured it all out. Mewling into the soft recesses of his mother's belly, he figured out what it was like to die. Blinking at the warm lights overhead, crossing his eyes until he felt dizzy, he wondered if he could believe what his pale green eyes saw. While brushing his teeth in the bathroom he stared at the wallpaper, the fleur-de-lis pattern a grey faded green. Did a mother's nipple taste the same—salty and warm and buttery—to his brother? Did we inhabit the same universe, or could we conjure one for ourselves? He pawed at his banana toy, yellow for now, but it could have been purple for all he knew, and he could tell himself that it was purple all along, all he would have to do is blink. It would change before him, he told himself, he could will it. He could master the universe. It was all right there. Just close your eyes and sleep.

EVERYTHING YOU DO

HANNAH STORM

You were 14. On school exchange in France, the cousin of your pen-friend trapped you in a toilet, tried to tear open the door with a knife. Your face reflected in the mirror, pale, and you imagined an animal frozen before the kill.

In French, *chasser* is to hunt. Now, you think of the word chase. He chased you. You were chaste. You did not know this word back then. But for years, you blamed yourself.

Earlier you danced with him, spinning beneath the disco ball to that song from Robin Hood. You leant in when he kissed you, teeth knocking his. His tongue found your mouth and you tried not to gag, wondering if happy ever afters were meant to feel this way.

Later when you broke free from the toilet, his family laughed. At the table laid with food in your honor, they bent their heads low and you did too to, pretending to pray. Then the father carved the meat and pointed to it blooming red across your plate and smiled.

"Sanglier," he said. You knew he hunted wild boar in the forest. Imagined Robin Hood and the arrow hurtling towards you and you wondered why Hollywood always had a happy ending. Now you know 'sang' means 'blood,' that prey is different from pray, that you have been one and done the other and that on both occasions nobody has heard you. In English 'Sang' is pronounced the same way as song. You think of the words again of that soundtrack to your first kiss, the promise of the title "Everything I Do: I Do it For You," and the lyrics. "I would give it all. I would sacrifice."

2021

For years you will be terrified of toilets, you will hold your breath when the door locks behind you and you will remember. You will think about everything you gave, everything you sacrificed.

You will wonder if the boy who did this to you understood the words to the song. You will remember the color of blood on the plate, the color of your face, blood-drained in the mirror. You will remember that 'no' sounds the same in both your languages.

LIGHTS

ANTHONY VARALLO

Table lamp, silver, with linen shade. 40-watt bulb, soft white:
What his sister tells him is that she needs someone to watch the kids while she picks up Mom from the hospital. Did he really think she was going to handle this all alone? If he wants to help out for once, she says, he'll tell Jessica the situation and get on the road. Like, now. He tells his sister he'll tell Jessica, but the truth is that Jessica hasn't shared his bed for months; she sleeps in the master bedroom, while he sleeps in the guest room, where they've relegated most of their least-loved furniture. Like this lamp, a leftover from Jessica's graduate school days. He observes its shade, his eyes adjusting to the light, and tells his sister he's on his way.

Ceiling fixture, kitchen, brushed nickel, 4-bulb:
It's just like her brother to sleep through a night like this, the sister thinks, with Dad in the hospital and Mom at the end of her rope. That's why she's moved back home, so she can help Mom deal with everything, while her brother is off in his own little world, like usual. She sits at the kitchen table and writes a list of things he can make the kids for breakfast, in the event that she and Mom aren't back in time. Outside, it is dark. She can see herself reflected in the sliding glass doors, haloed by the kitchen light.

Car headlights, sealed beam bulbs, clear, halogen, 35 watts:
If his sister would ever listen to him, he thinks, as he drives the backroads to his parents' house, she might pick up on the fact that his marriage is falling apart. How can she not tell? But, then again, how could she,

when she's so wrapped up in Dad's health problems, in Mom's fears and worries, in addition to raising two kids as a single mom. Still, to act like he's letting everyone down, when he's the one driving thirty miles in the middle of the night to watch her kids. Someone should make him a cape, he thinks, then realizes he's actually just said this aloud, to the steering wheel, to the radio, to the front windshield, where the headlights offer up the occasional deer, watching from the shoulder of the road.

Nightlight, upstairs hallway, Snoopy-themed:
She doesn't think the kids will wake this late at night, but you never know. The nightlight is from her childhood, probably an electrical hazard of some kind or another. Still, it works. That old doghouse. That familiar glow.

iPhone 8, 4.7-inch screen display, brightness: medium:
When he gets Jessica's text—where r u?—he can't exactly respond to it in detail. He holds the phone at steering wheel level and manages to text Becca called. Driving. Parents' house. He thinks about adding more, but what else is there to say? A car, approaching in the distance, switches its high beams off.

Parking lot lights, LED, 80-watt, occasional flickering:
Hard to believe, but she still has to search for a parking place in the hospital lot, even at this time of night. Day, she should say. Early morning. Either way, she's got to hold it together for Mom, who is not terribly great at holding it together, which only upsets Dad even more, as she's reminded Mom a thousand times. She rehearses the look she will turn on Mom when Mom turns a look on her that says, Who is it that can tell me how to be? She is good at this look, has used it several times in the past few days, whenever Dad's health plays keep-away with them. Walking across the lot, she thinks she hears cicadas in the trees, then realizes it's the lights, thrumming, clearing their radiant throats.

Porch light, 3-bulb, black finish, steel frame:
She's left the key under the mat, foolishly, but it's probably OK at this time of night, he figures. The lock resists the key at first, and he wonders why

Dad hasn't gotten around to loosening the lock with graphite, the way he always did, and then it hits him that he's grown now, and his marriage is over, and Dad is probably dying, and what does the door lock matter now?

Fluorescent light, 32-watt, 2-light, single cord:
Mom's look is all she needs to know. She goes to her, and then to Dad, whose eyes are closed in the unflattering light.

6-inch mounted hallway light, bronze finish:
From the front hallway he can see into the kitchen, where someone has left the overhead light on, and where can barely glimpse a note on the kitchen table, pinned beneath a ballpoint pen. In his sister's scrupulous script, no doubt. He closes the front door behind him, locks it, quietly. And that's when he hears the kids at the top of the stairs.

Lighted keypad, Trimline phone, white, wall-mounted:
Between sobs, his sister tells him the news. He says, Oh no. Says, How's Mom? Says, Oh no. Says, I will. Says, Actually, they're already up.

Ceiling fixture, kitchen, brushed nickel, 4-bulb:
Why is he here? Who is on the phone? Where is their mommy? Why is he crying? To these questions, he has an answer, and that answer is: he reads the note, then takes a bowl from the cabinet, grabs flour, baking powder and oil from the pantry, and milk and eggs from the fridge. He's here to make them breakfast, he tells them. What else? The kids give him sleepy, skeptical looks at first, but then he finds the chocolate chips and their faces light up.

BIOACOUSTICS

MEGAN STOLZ

Did you dip your head beneath
Pacific coastal waters to hear

the whale symphony? Do they call
back across the land miles to home?

We have a humming tectonic rumble,
unheard by human ears but felt

every year. Your figure in the corner
of the choir, across the sections, my voice

sweetens with surety. We harmonize, improvise, carry
the other's melody before it's safe

to hand back. I memorize the feeling
of singing your song in my muscles to hum

in the deep winter. The waves of sound move
ocean waters, pausing for peace when needed

in the noise. We can stand in silence and hold
hands, listening to each other.

For Katie McKee

Source materials:

- Giggs, R. (2019). Whale Songs Are Getting Deeper. [online] Available at: https://www.theatlantic.com/magazine/archive/2019/10/whale-songs-are-getting-deeper/596635/ [Accessed 3 March 2020].
- Monterey Bay Aquarium Research Institute (MBARI) (2018). Humpback whale song from Monterey Bay. Available at: https://www.youtube.com/watch?v=5tRMqbPH_pk [Accessed 3 Mar. 2020].
- Whale & Dolphin Conservation USA. (2020). Facts about whales – Whale & Dolphin Conservation USA. [online] Available at: https://us.whales.org/whales-dolphins/facts-about-whales/ [Accessed 3 Mar. 2020].

ALL THE THINGS WE CAN'T SAY, WE TAP INSTEAD

CHELSEA STICKLE

The year Kelly's mom died was the year she taught me Morse code. At night under the covers of the double bed we shared she instructed by touching my skin. She mouthed letters in the beginning to get me going. Her fingers tap tap tapped on my forearm, my thigh. Short short short short / short short. Hi. There was only room in my brain for the letter on the tip of her tongue. Pink perfection.

All tapping was code, and Kelly had plenty to say about her mom's death, the absence of cute boys and her inevitable move to Fort Meade at the end of summer to live with her dad. Until then she was all mine. We slept in the same bed and woke up with our limbs tangled together like ragdolls. Brushed each other's hair and messed around with makeup. They were molasses days full of bike rides around town, VHS tapes from Blockbuster, and popsicles under the umbrella of the willow tree followed by Morse code practice with the leftover sticks.

Whenever my parents entered our room, which was any room we were in, we switched to code. Kelly was grieving so they didn't push her to talk, and that made her even more mine. I was the one she could talk to. I was the other half of the Double Pop. Without her I had a jagged edge running down my side. My mom reminded me that Kelly had to leave soon. She bought us friendship lamps that were linked so when I touched my lamp, hers would glow, too.

The day Kelly left, I pressed the gift into her hands and tapped to say, "So you'll know when I'm thinking about you." Her dad yelled for her to hurry up, and the pretzel twist on her face made me think she couldn't listen and hear at the same time. She told me she'd call me. I could barely eat anything other than popsicles during the first week. Chewing took too much energy, and my stomach roiled with all the sugar. I stayed curled up in the bed we shared, huffing her pillow, convinced the green apple shampoo lingered, and trying to remember what it was like when I was her shadow. I glanced over at the friendship lamp on my bedside table. We hadn't used the lamps since she first plugged hers in. But that afternoon hope overpowered the fear of loss, and my hands tapped out "I love you" in Morse code. She would finally know. The lamp only glowed once. She could see I was thinking about her but had no idea what that meant.

SHIPWRECKED

JAMY BOND

We are walking along the coast of Ilha de Mozambique, passing carcasses of old pirate ships parked in the sand. The moon hangs on its black cord above. *This is the island of ghost ships,* you say, *decay can be beautiful.* We are feeding peaches to bush babies in a Swazi game park: *Take my hand,* you say, *we'll drink wine by the beehive huts.* The moon disappears and it starts to rain. I cover you with my tarp but you push it away, hold out your arms, turn up your face, *let the sky kiss my flesh,* you say. I reach for the wet waves in your hair and whisper: *You'll be dead in a month.* You put a finger to my lips, *Shhh, we aren't supposed to know yet.* I am weeping to a white-coated doctor: *Vicodin, Percocet, Morphine. Give me anything. But where is the pain,* he asks, *can you point to it?* Your boyfriend is sobbing through the crackle of a land line: *I tried to save her; there was blood and glass everywhere.* In my dream, you sail through the windshield in a swan dive, glass glittering like diamonds around your face. Your broken wrists are wishbones of white in the night. We sit beneath a blanket of blue Jacarunda, eating pastries filled with prawns and cream. *I remember how you cared for me when we were kids,* you say, *after Dad left and Mom locked herself away; you held me after the nightmares.* On the skin above my breast, raw blisters emerge, broiling with pus, their crusty strings like arrows aimed at my heart. *The pain is right here,* I point for the doctor. *Please, make it go away.* My daughter is gathering sandstones into the folds of her t-shirt. I see you in the delicate curve of her jawbone as we creep through a Kruger forest to the glistening pale of a watering hole where lions stir in the morning mist. *Be very quiet,* you say with your eyes, *they can hear everything.* I would give anything to hold your hand, to lace my fingers with yours once again, but it is my daughter's hand reaching back as we walk through a field of bluebells, pine branches bending in the breeze, eagles circling overhead. It starts to rain. I pull her jacket closed, but she pushes my hand away. *I like the rain drops on my skin,* she says. She wants to be a surgeon when she grows up. *Did you know they can transplant an entire face?* She asks. *Peel it from me and stitch it to you.* She comes to me at night, crying from a dream, *we were shipwrecked and drowning at sea.* I reach for the snowy ringlets in her hair. *Tell me about nice things,* she says, slipping under the blanket, her heartbeat fast and shallow next to mine. *Once, two sisters wandered the ruins of limestone villas on the Island of Mozambique.* I say. *Were they pirates?* She asks. *Pioneers,* I say. She looks up at me and grins, but it's you I see smiling from the folds of her face, you I feel beating in the blood rhythm of my heart.

LANGUAGE ACQUISITION

ESHANI SURYA

This is the story I ask my mother to repeat: how I, a wet-lipped babe in my grandmother's Bihari home, forgot all the English words I'd collected for a few years in just a month.

This is the part I embellish a little: my uncle, bringing his—maybe handsome, like well-kempt goats—Kingfisher beer-scented, gold pendant Ganesh-wearing friends to the house to play carrom board into the night.

This is my mother's punchline: my uncle wanted to show me off, this talented niece from America, and he asked me to say something, anything, in English, but I just chirruped *kya bolu, kya bolu,* hoping he'd give me something to parrot back, but he had nothing and I had nothing and still neither did he, except sending me to the mosquito-webbing swathed bed, both of us disappointed and laughing.

This is mine: back in America I was exotic too and a white boy at the church nursery school asked me to say something in Hindi over the fragmented playdough and I placed my sweaty hands on my cheeks and said *what should I say* and he said *just one word, can't you do that* and the safest, most kindred phrase seemed to be dog, so I said it, flat and tremory—*kuth-tha*—and the white boy scoffed a little at that, as if he didn't believe me, so I said it again, bark bark, on command.

TWO POEMS (DA FUGUE ZONE: VOL #37 AND VOL #86)

JOE HALL

Da Fugue Zone Vol #37: Stock Keeping Unit

fugue, all you said we could do was dodge through
one more day without hurting someone
in our panic looking through the ventricles of the city
the spirals and eyelets, the long-fingered clasp
days passed like rain or vapor from the dryer
where you put before us a meal, a steaming
tray, heaped with knuckles
would I say I was deskilled
in a long now of stocking shelves
would I say I had misplaced so much life
the sun breathes, massive, obliterating
who knew how to hold themselves
how to hold their ache, who knew
the oil of fugue in a bottle cap by the fan
the laces of bus routes in the grievance file of heaven
there it always is
in Da Fugue Zone
the Fugue Zone #37

Da Fugue Zone Vol #86: Poor Food Baloney

my kid baloney anomie deep in the mist down where couches slouch
in the mind, where to be less lonely, mix milk w/water
w/I don't have any money to mother
and now must eat what I have pictured
dear power, dear reader, we'll change
who we are won't meet
dear mist,
dear vapor burning off into
the long hall of this life, the sleeves
of saltines, my tongue's rasp across salt,
corrugated edges, I could stand straight up
in peanut butter, add a roof
we ate sugar

on toast, butter between two
slices, ketchup w/o eggs
the days' yolk bleeds across calendar squares
summer storms break across this house
but only, it seems, when we are curled in sleep
and a chord hangs in the air
the full unhurried note
before the bottom falls out
dear friend,

what was I afraid of?
what I was always afraid of, I could see
how well you loved yourself
tho you, too, never had much

FATHER'S FABRIC

XUEYI ZHOU

Father was folding a pile of Polo imitations, emerald with electric yellow logos yelling POST OFFICE. These were not real Polos, but nylon uniforms he stole from the factory's warehouse, whose guard would feign amnesia for a loosie. He folded them into blocks, sized as the one-yuan tofu we bought from the market for dinner, and put them into the freezer. Allegedly, the coldness would peel off the prints, then I could wear them outside without fear. No proof no crime was his logic; just a small convenience for a textile man. Hours later, he reopened the T-shirts and found the prints stubborn, so he flipped out his penknife and started scraping. He sat hunched on the stool, his cigarette and sweat glowing, and the plastisol rained down like fluorescent fish scales.

He always smelt like smoked mackerel, a hard sell that took me years to get used to, and that night I thought to myself: if he could quit and cleanse and wear fancy colognes, maybe mother would have stayed. When I woke up the next morning, father was already in the factory for his morning shift, loading clothes into industrial washers and dryers. The skin of the emerald T-shirts had been cleaned up, all seven of them. I put one on. He had marked them with stitches, Monday to Sunday, and a faint smell of tobacco.

I grew in oversized male T-shirts, wearing them as nightdresses, grew out of them, then in fake Nike hoodies, Levi's sweaters, Tommy Hilfiger dresses. For a summer I only wore tie-dyed T-shirts of explosive color clashes, like neon green with bright blue or pink with purple—it was the fad overseas and father was tying white tees day and night. The following two years I wore jeans ripped open manually with electric spinning wheels. One day a worker fell asleep and the wheels ate three of his fingers. The jeans became history. If that textile man saw the punk jeans in the stores, would he stroke his deboned wounds and be surprised by how soft they were? One of the nameless hidden prices behind the mass production of machine washables, the clothes my mother despised.

Her body wanted something delicate enough that transcended machine washing, so she left us to keep her aspiration alive. But the machine washables warmed me. They stayed rough and tired but stayed.

By the time I got to the real Polos, the ones with carefully embroidered emblems, the factory owner suddenly laid off everyone. Diagnosed with heart disease, the owner decided to close for good. At the dismissal meeting, the owner stressed that he was sorry, but he was old and tired, and he wanted to rest. Father and the other workers, all middle-aged or above, listened with sadness, not for the owner's health but for their absence of a future. After the owner drove away in his imported Maserati, the textile men scattered into the corners of other factories sniffing for jobs. Father grabbed a bulky bag of Polo shirts to take with him; a fair compensation.

He waited for me to come home with a cupful of cigarette butts and the needle with the biggest eye.

I threaded it, and his needle swam up and down, sewing the buttons on. "Aren't you bored with these old man's T-shirts anyway?" he asked as he burned the loose threads with his lighter. "I know a factory that makes linens for chain hotels. Do you prefer florals or solid colors?" He forced a smile when he looked up, but the needle bit his thumb. He put it in his mouth and ducked my gaze, his shoulders slightly trembling. I hugged him from the back and said that linen sounded great; we would get much more fabric than T-shirts and jeans. Then I took over the needle, wiped off the blood, and carried on sewing.

THE LION'S TOOTH

RACHEL KOWALSKY

The lion had a cavity, and the veterinarian was trying to pull his tooth. But something was wrong—the tooth was stuck, or maybe what Aunt May said was true, and the vet on the animal show wasn't strong enough to wrestle it from his jaw.

I felt ashamed for her, a tiny blonde woman. Aunt May kept calling her the *female* vet, as in the *female* vet can't pull the tooth.

That's why I went running. I chose a quiet path and I ran fast, for a long time. The trees grew tall around me, casting longer and longer shadows as the sun dropped in the sky.

At dark I noticed footsteps behind me, matching my rhythm and pace. When I sped up the footsteps did too. When I turned north, their steady pulse followed. I stopped running and leaned against a tree trunk; all fell silent.

***

A nurse whispered "I'm Abby" and then she shouted, *I need help in triage*, after which a lot more people came running. They pushed my stretcher into a large room with shining equipment attached to the walls. Somebody with a rolling voice said "Her vitals are OK" and somebody with an accent I couldn't place said "sexual a-ssault" and then Abby said "She has to go to room ten," although I didn't go anywhere just yet. There were wires and cables being shuffled and untangled and attached to me, a needle in my arm. I asked if I was dying and they all said "No!" There was an x-ray, the warm rush of morphine, the flash of a needle and thread at the edge of my vision, and more morphine. Finally someone helped me stand up and walk because we were going to room ten. Abby walked next to me.

I could open my eyes a little; I was wearing a hospital gown and some hospital socks. They were thin but the treads were good so I didn't lose my footing on the gleaming floors.

We walked down a hallway lined with sliding doors. At its end was an old-fashioned wooden door, the sort you'd see on a Tudor, with a stained-glass window. Abby nodded towards the door, so I opened it, revealing a flight of stairs.

I began to climb.

It's a good thing I'm a runner because there were a lot of stairs. After the first hundred or so, I started sweating, and I asked Abby how many more I had to climb. "All of them," she said. There were no landings, only stairs. But I kept going.

I thought about the straight, flat timeline of my life. Before today, it contained only one event—my mother leaving me with Aunt May—and that was a long time ago. Since then I hadn't done much except learn that I was good at mathematics and running. Today seemed to ruin the line, make its continuation impossible. I was glad to be climbing. When we reached the top, we pushed through a heavy metal door and emerged on the roof of the hospital.

Abby walked in front of me, stopped at the X of the helipad, and unfurled a thick blanket with a snap of her wrists. The free edge sailed up then collapsed obediently, its clear green a surprise against the grit of the roof. "This is your room," she said. I stepped onto the soft blanket, a luxury. Then I lay down and took a few deep breaths.

Abby sat next to me. She reached to the side and picked up a white cardboard box a bit bigger than a shoe box, then pulled a scissor from her pocket and slit open the seal so the lid sprang open; when she did that a bunch of papers fluttered out and flew away on the wind.

Everywhere around me I could see lights. Not just the stars; there were glowing lamps or candles or fireflies in every window. The entire city shone with light.

Abby rummaged through the white box. Her hair was unreasonably long; it was piled around her in thick, bright waves of red and gold, and her neck and shoulders were lean cords poking out of her scrubs. Here was a truly strong woman, I thought, one who could pull the lion's tooth like a weed from the earth.

She took my hand in hers and cleaned my nails. Soil came out from under them in heaps, landing with soft thuds and thumps on the blanket. She pulled envelopes from her box and began to fill them, then seal and label them: "Bay leaf. Celery. Turmeric. Thyme." She combed my hair and picked the leaves out of it and washed my body, then she filled up envelopes that said *Stephanie's shining hair* and *From Stephanie's running legs* and *From Stephanie's wonderful pumping arms.*

I lay quietly under the stars, wondering what else was out there besides space trash and asteroids.

* * *

Maybe room ten was not a room, but a world. Maybe it was a metaphor for this world. Or maybe room ten was my body, its inside and outside, filled with searchlights that blinked slowly on and off.

The sky was changing. Orange light filtered through the clouds to the east; now I could see all the way to the city's outskirts. The buildings blurred and receded, yielding green mountains and a rushing riverbed that wound its way through.

Abby handed me my running shoes. "Lace up," she said. I understood that I had to run again.

It was hard. First of all, my feet against the earth brought back the terror of my earlier run, and also my stomach hurt. My head ached and my neck was stiff. But I kept going.

I gained speed as I went. My legs moved and my arms pumped. My heart pumped and my lungs moved behind my ribcage. My ribs ached. I heard footsteps behind me.

I ran faster, turning down an intersecting path, but the footsteps followed me. I turned off the path and ran across a field, I ducked into a stand of trees and weaved through them with pine needles muffling my footsteps, but still I heard muffled steps behind me. I skidded down a muddy bank and plunged through icy water. I scrambled up the other side but the footsteps pursued me.

Finally I stood up tall, a firmly rooted tree in a stand of pines beneath a vast sky. The sky was orange gold. Its beauty wasn't lost on me.

"What do you want?" I asked.

It was Abby. She was breathing hard, covered in mud, one hand steadying her against a tree. Panting, she held the other hand out to me, palm up. She had the lion's tooth. I came close, to really see the thing. It was smooth and shiny with blood at the root and a black cavity at its center, foul with rot and decay.

* * *

We celebrated Aunt May's seventy-second birthday last night, just the two of us and a lemon cake. After the cake she turned on the vet show again; this time it was about a dog who lost his leg in a raccoon trap. "What a pity," she said. "Such a helpless creature."

I went to bed early and woke at midnight to the lion standing beside my bed, his great pink nose an inch from my face, his eyes amber-green and remote.

I raised myself up on an elbow and held his gaze, which was quiet and not unfriendly. He was, I could see, a creature like me: subject to pain and pestilence, shot through with a bit of the divine.

* * *

He turned away and padded around the room, sniffing at my socks and shoes, the mess of papers on the floor where I scribble and scrawl my story. Words are reliable allies. They hold the story for me.

The lion. I was sure he had come for the tooth, but it was mine to carry. After Aunt May picked me up from the hospital, I'd cleaned and polished the thing, cut it down to size and scrubbed its center clean. Then I tucked it into my wrist, right next to the pulse, so the blood rushes by it with each beat. *I feel it move when I run*, I told him, silently. *Like a splinter or a tiny engine, every time my feet touch the earth.*

SOCIAL TIME

APRIL BRADLEY

It's social time on the psych unit, and as we play cards, I tell the 16-year-old girl next to me what to expect with her abortion. A thought peeks around the corner of my mind—my mother was this girl's very age when she had me. I examine her skin. It's luminous, flawless. It's a detail I'll recall years from now when I understand the fact that she is a hallucination, an aberrant sensory experience—a living dream. Here, and in my memory, she fills up space with her presence. And yet everything I could ever wish to know about her lives within my own mind. She's so young, it hurts to look at her.

I describe the clinic but don't tell her it's run down, that the fluorescent lighting will illuminate the waiting room like a morgue, that when it's quiet, she'll hear a high-pitched electronic whistle, that the buzzing will contribute to the surreality of her lonely situation. I warn her about protesters and use generic words like *graphic* and *manipulative* and *deceptive* because I can't bring myself to tell this girl how good Christian people will spew rage through bullhorns as they parade-pray gargantuan photos of mutilated fetuses. Instead, I mention the clinic's bulletproof glass at the entrance and detail the workup routine a typical patient hears.

"Yes, it will hurt," I confide when she asks. I wish I could pay for her anesthesia, but I'm on Medicaid and can't imagine ever having enough money to fund other women's abortions. I wish I could call the clinic director, and later I do, from the patient's phone in the hallway. I want to say, hey, if this girl can't afford Twilight, let me pay for it, but I don't. I advise the director to expect her, to attend to the girl herself, not hand her over to an artless intern. That's the word I use, *artless*. I twirl the phone cord and think about how this unit could use some art therapy. The director offers me my old job. She says I was the best abortion counselor she ever trained. I'm not exactly sure when I'm available to work because my voluntary admission to the psychiatric hospital feels supremely involuntary. I don't like how the olanzapine affects me but I've learned about the consequences of non-compliance from other patients. Besides, I have an infant at home and it's time for my Narcotics Anonymous meeting. NA's where I exchange my recent experiences with blood clots and intense anxiety and expansive psychosis for harrowing ones about opioid addiction.

I ask the girl if she's sure. I have no idea what's going on with her, except she is here like me—slotted in among the sympathetic heroin addicts on the dual diagnosis unit due to a lack of beds on the women's ward. She's the youngest on the floor, everyone's little sister, and years later when I'm visiting the children and adolescent unit, I'll wonder why she wasn't admitted there until my brain stutters, and I'll remind myself that she's not real. But then and there, what preoccupies me is whether her consent is diminished or wholly subsumed. There's no way to know how medicated she is or if she comprehends what she's agreed to. I don't tell her police will escort her to the clinic in shackles all the way to the threshold of the procedure room. I don't tell her the director will have to shame the officers into removing her shackles the same way I did for another patient in similar circumstances. I don't tell her that no woman should have an abortion handcuffed and in chains. It hasn't occurred to this girl that she will be treated like a criminal for being sick. If she is. Ill, that is—mentally ill. Could be that she's just a teenager. And I wonder, where is her mother? Does her mother know what's going on? My hallucination never receives visitors.

The girl continues to play cards with me and appears relaxed; she makes eye contact with me, makes small talk, smiles. She asks me what I know about electroconvulsive therapy, and everything I know is literary. She shows me a pamphlet with dated graphics, and I'm reminded of ads from medical journals in the 1960s. Do I know anything about it? Should she do it? I tell her to try everything else first. I think of Sylvia Plath and how maybe some Prozac could have saved her brilliant life and I wonder if something will save my lackluster one. I hear a baby crying and I see a couple of the staff dragging the struggling girl away to solitary where I hear patients lie on gurneys in restraints. My milk should be letting down, but it's not. I try to ignore the baby's cries and concentrate on the girl because she is here again sitting beside me, nodding her head and saying "yeah" or calling me *April* with smooth vowels like my mother's voice, saying my name exactly the way my mother does. Her hair is long with soft-looking curls. She has freckles and hazel eyes like my mother. My baby cries and cries and my heart races. I can't breathe because my baby continues to cry and cry and cry. Her need me fills up, floods my body. I can't reach her. I shout to the nurse across the room, interrupting the girl, "Is my baby here? Where is my baby? Is this real?" *How can any of this be real?*

Once again, I am alone. The nurse points to the television and says, "It's real."

THE BURYING KIND

B. TYLER LEE

Y ou're dead today, and I want to write something insightful about
toadstool shadows in the park, something about ants trudging in
line, something tying the domain of the earthbound and gleaming
to you, but all I can think of is the month you spent battering my will
until I gave in and let you push inside me where I didn't want you to—
"outgoing mail only," I'd said, because I loathe shit and the idea of that
part of me stretching open, pain in a place where pain belongs but not
that kind, how the wrong pain in a place you expect to hurt can be worse
than a surprise ache where you thought there was none—and when I said
I wouldn't do that again, after I shrieked and crushed my eyelids together
and almost puked, you still begged until weeks later, when, nine Malibu
and Diet Cokes in, I said, "If you're going to do it, now's the time, I can't
feel much," and so you did, and it hurt more than rum told me it would,
but you kept thrusting, snot and tears and snot down my face and my
neck until you came inside a shuddering body that learned volumes about
you in that moment, and it feels, today, like I should be able to spin a tren-
chant metaphor re: goose shit in this park, but I keep remembering how
later, after we'd broken up, you got drunk in bars across from the English
building and breathed to our grad classmates one by one, *B. likes anal.*
That's what does it for her, and the thing here is I wouldn't have minded
had that been true, wouldn't care if you'd broadcast my basest cravings as
sport; what I hated (the wrong type of pain rocked up in your highball
glass) was watching you try to humiliate me—and it worked, because how
do you defend yourself in such a case without degrading someone's else

desire, without seeming to protest too much?—and goddammit, I ache to recover whatever kernel of love you must've cradled for me the afternoon you opened a circular and pointed out the 10k bands that would shine best on my ring finger; I can't recall anything kind, but there must've been tacos and calla lilies and jazz clubs that compelled me to stay, made me arch my back every time you requested it, built me a wish you'd shovel bits of yourself into this gaping inside me—the void that keeps me clinging to those nights of vomiting merlot in a red rayon slip dress on the shoulder of Loop 12 as if they meant *any*thing, and now, sprawled like I'm nine Solo cups in though I'm 3:00 PM sober, bawling in the warm dirt of these woods, I don't care you're dead because if you'd seen me for even a second, you'd have realized the only thing you needed to know:

    My kink is filling
    the wet, wormy hole of my
    own limitless shame.

(SEVERE THUNDERSTORMS)

CHRISTOPHE CASAMASSIMA

ii.

I start a fire to keep warm
inhale the mentholated hearth
but you rain down hard
with your condescending lightening

and by sheer coincidence, I find myself
—every time!—outside the Gallerie d'Orvalle
—when it rains!—and so my aesthetic
education comes with a little drip of the nose
—not a cold!—but under the Ghiberti,
the smiling Uccello, the Sibiu Crucifixion
—all reproductions!—I shed a tear
a real tear, for Ghirlandaio's Birth of Saint John the Baptist
crumpling a little, at the center, where Elisabeth
looks down upon the newborn prefix and his nurses
—garlands, outstretched hands, and fruit—so much fruit!—
not without some exhaustion, efficient grace, where no one
has noticed the water pooling at her bosom—O Titian!
where are you now with your assumptive flying virgins!

ODE TO A SIBLING

EMILY FRANKLIN

You—the undertaker
of my shadow days
collecting bodies of old
insects that crawled into
our tent made of refrigerator
boxes, the cardboard sturdy
enough to hold us for as long
as one season, wallpapered,
colored, window flaps waving—

you are the funeral host
of days we cannot get back,
each one encrusted with something
one of us has misremembered or
exaggerated unintentionally as though
we are trying to sell our childhoods to
each other even though neither of us
can afford buying them back. If we
could, would you look into the coffin,
lift the lid and see remains—
houses, dogs, invalid keys, those letters
we exchanged, determined each
to have one permanent address

and now you are the keeper
of each imperfect tense, all that had
been and all the was to have been and
all that we don't even know will be
as your children and mine slip through
their days unaware they are accumulating
losses just by waking up with last night
scrubbed out. We have each made them
siblings and for that there is a Hebrew blessing—
the older shall serve the younger
rav ya'avod tza'ir so you have been my undertaker
and will—I hope—continue, but know this, too, I am yours.

2022

SUNDAY MORNING VISITATION

KATIE KEMPLE

Dad lives in a donut shop now,
the parchment wings flying
down to meet the cruller I select.

He's the warmth of the cheap
coffee, its bitter tang
meant for sugar and cream.

I drink it black, back in my car,
lid off, dipping the hollow
pastry in torn chunks into

brown metallic sauce. The way
I'm sure Dad must
have done, alone in his car

to avoid Mom's brutal jabs
at his eating habits.
He wasn't happy to outlive

her. I took after him, doughy
and soft in the center,
despite Mom's molding—

2022

never could meet a donut
I didn't like. But I'll visit
her next, at ballet class, kicking

the shit out of air, with Dad's
blood leaping in my veins,
the two of them duking it out,

making my pulse rush. Until,
empty cup and slippers flung
off, I fold my sugared wings.

CONTRIBUTOR BIOS

C.J.A. is a poet, critic, essayist, and current PhD candidate at the University of Southern California. Their work has appeared in numerous journals including *ZYZZYVA, Southwest Review, Denver Quarterly,* and *Columbia Journal.* They live in Los Angeles. Read more at cjapoet.com.

Margaret Adams's work has appeared in *The Best Small Fictions 2019, Threepenny Review, Joyland Magazine, The Pinch Journal,* and *Monkeybicycle,* among other publications

Anthony Aguero is a queer writer in Los Angeles, CA. His work has appeared, or will appear, in the *Bangalore Review, 2River View, The Acentos Review, The Temz Review, Rhino Poetry, Cathexis Northwest Press, 14 Poems, Redivider Journal, Maudlin House,* and others.

Nancy Allen is a criminal defense attorney, yoga studio owner, and yoga teacher, swimmer, and poet living in the Virginia mountains. You'll find her in the James River all summer long and in front of the wood stove all winter. She has been published in several journals, including *Tar River Poetry, Sow's Ear River, Gargoyle,* and *JMWW.*

Jessie Lovett Allen is originally from western New York and currently teaches English at North Platte Community College in western Nebraska. Recent work appears or is forthcoming in *Best Small Fictions 2022, Milk Candy Review, The Forge, NCTE English Journal,* and *JMWW.*

Frances Badgett is the fiction editor of *Contrary Magazine*. Her work has appeared in *SmokeLong Quarterly, Anomaly (formerly Drunken Boat), Word Riot, Matchbook*, and elsewhere. Her work has made the Wigleaf 50 longlist, been included in *2019 Best Small Fictions*, and nominated for a Pushcart Prize. Her website is francesbadgett.com. Her Instagram is FrancesBad. Her Twitter is francesbadgett.

Clare Banks is associate editor of *Smartish Pace*. A Maryland State Arts Council Independent Artist Award Winner, her poems have appeared in *Poetry South, Poet Lore*, and *Mississippi Review*, among other journals. Nominated for Best New Poets 2022, she lives in Baltimore City with her family.

Tyler Barton is the author of *Eternal Night at the Nature Museum* (Sarabande Books, 2021), and *The Quiet Part Loud* (Split Lip, 2019). Stories have appeared in *Electric Literature, Kenyon Review, Iowa Review*, and elsewhere. He leads writing workshops for the elderly in assisted living facilities and for incarcerated individuals in the Adirondack Mountains of NY. Find him @goftyler or tsbarton.com

Lisa Bass lives in California with her family, including three daughters. She writes poems and short prose, and studies and teaches at The Writer's Studio. Her piece "un/synced" was an Editor's Choice selection in *Craft* (2021).

Aileen Bassis is a poet and visual artist in New York City. She was awarded two residencies in poetry to Atlantic Center for the Arts. Two of her poems appear in anthologies about migration. Her journal publications include *Spillway, Grey Sparrow Journal, Canary, The Pinch, Prelude* and *The Southampton Review.*

Krys Malcolm Belc is the author of the memoir *The Natural Mother of the Child* (Counterpoint) and the flash nonfiction chapbook *In Transit* (The Cupboard Pamphlet.) He is the memoir editor of *Split Lip Magazine* and lives with his partner and their three young children in Philadelphia.

Roy Bentley, a finalist for the Miller Williams prize, has published ten books of poetry. His work has appeared in magazines, including *Shenandoah, North American Review, Crazyhorse, The Southern Review, New Ohio Review, december,* and *Prairie Schooner,* among others. His latest collection, *Beautiful Plenty,* is available from Main Street Rag.

Donald Berger is the author of *The Long Time,* a bilingual edition in English and German (Wallstein Press, Goettingen, Germany), *Quality Hill* (Lost Roads Publishers) and *The Cream-Filled Muse* (Fledermaus Press). His poems and prose have appeared in *The New Republic, Slate, Conjunctions,* and other magazines including some from Berlin, Leipzig, Budapest, Hong Kong, and mainland China. He currently teaches at Johns Hopkins University.

Jamy Bond's stories and essays have appeared in a variety of publications, including *Pithead Chapel, JMWW, The Forge Literary Magazine, Barren Magazine, wigleaf, The Sun Magazine,* and *The Rumpus.* She earned her MFA from George Mason University and lives in Washington, DC

Rebecca Bornstein is a poet and worker who's held many jobs– including production cook, elementary school secretary, goat sitter, and creative writing instructor. She's the recipient of a 2022 Oregon Literary Fellowship, and her poetry has appeared *in Tinderbox Poetry Journal, The Baltimore Review, The Boiler, The Journal,* and elsewhere.

April Bradley is a Durham, North Carolina-based writer. Her fiction and essays appear in *CRAFT Literary, Narratively,* and *Smokelong Quarterly,* among others. She is the editor of *Ruby* and a graduate of Eckerd College and Yale Divinity School. She and her husband, John, live part-time on their sailboat, Daily Alice.

Aaron Brown is the author most recently of Call Me Exile (SFASU Press 2022). He has published work in *Image, World Literature Today, Tupelo Quarterly, Waxwing,* and *Transition,* among others. Brown grew up in

Chad and now lives in Texas, where he is an assistant professor of English at LeTourneau University.

Caroliena Cabada's fiction has been published in *Barren Magazine, jmww,* and was selected for *Best Small Fictions 2021.* She teaches first-year composition at the University of Nebraska-Lincoln, where she is earning her PhD in English.

Nicole Callihan writes poems and stories. Her books include *SuperLoop, The Deeply Flawed Human,* and *ELSEWHERE* (with Zoë Ryder White). Her work has appeared or is forthcoming in *Kenyon Review, Colorado Review, Conduit, The American Poetry Review,* and as a Poem-a-Day selection from the Academy of American Poets. Learn more at www. nicolecallihan.com.

Christophe Casamassima is the managing director of the Baltimore Poetry Library at Towson University, which consists of roughly 6,000 volumes and objects. He is also the founder/publisher of Furniture Press Books in Baltimore, and the author of five collections of poetry, including the *Mostly Surfaces* (SubPress, 2022), and *Totems* (New Materialist Press, 2023).

Emily Cementina received an M.F.A. in Fiction from The New School, and graduated from NYU with a B.A. in Dramatic Literature. Her writing has appeared online at *Juked, jmww, THRUSH,* and *fwriction : review.* She is an adjunct lecturer of Creative Writing at St. Joseph's University in Brooklyn, NY.

Laura Huey Chamberlain lives, works, and writes in Alexandria, Virginia. Her fiction has appeared in journals including *Hobart, jmww, MoonPark Review,* and *Cease, Cows.* She was a finalist for the 2019 Best Microfiction.

Barbara Daniels's *Talk to the Lioness* was published by Casa de Cinco Hermanas Press. She received four fellowships from the New Jersey State

Council on the Arts. Her poetry has appeared in *Permafrost, Westchester Review, Philadelphia Stories, Coachella Review*, and many other journals.

Alexandra Daley holds a Bachelor's degree in creative writing from College of Charleston. Her poetry has appeared in several publications, including *Crazyhorse, Emerge, FLARE: The Flaglar Review*, and *The Oklahoma Review*. She currently lives in Charleston, SC, with her husband and three labs.

Marc Darnell is a lead custodian and online tutor in Omaha, Nebraska, and received his MFA from the University of Iowa. He *has been published in The Lyric, Blue Unicorn, The Journal of Undiscovered Poets, Verse-Virtual, The Literary Nest, The Pangolin Review*, and elsewhere.

Tommy Dean is the author of two flash fiction chapbooks *Special Like the People on TV* (Redbird Chapbooks, 2014) and *Covenants* (ELJ Editions, 2021). *Hollows*, was published by Alternating Current Press in 2022. He is the Editor at *Fractured Lit* and *Uncharted Magazine*. Find him at tommydeanwriter.com and on Twitter @TommyDeanWriter.

Oliver de la Paz is the author of six books of poetry including *The Boy in the Labyrinth* (University of Akron Press) and *The Diaspora Sonnets* (Liveright Press 2023). He teaches at the College of the Holy Cross and in the Low Residency MFA Program at PLU.

Monica Dickson is a short fiction writer from Leeds, UK. Her work has appeared in *Spelk, Anti-Heroin Chic, X-R-A-Y*, and elsewhere. Her story 'Receipts' made the inaugural BIFFY 50 list. She is a 2021 graduate of the Northern Short Story Festival Academy. More at writingandthelike.wordpress.com and on Twitter @Mon_Dickson

Michael Diebert is the author of *Thrash* (Brick Road, 2022) and *Life Outside the Set* (Sweatshoppe, 2022). He teaches writing and literature at Perimeter College, Georgia State University and previously served as poetry editor for *The Chattahoochee Review*. Recent poems appear in *Another Chicago Magazine* and *River Teeth* and are forthcoming in *EcoTheo Review*. A two-time cancer survivor, Michael lives in Avondale Estates, Georgia with his wife and dogs.

Yasmina Din Madden is a Vietnamese American writer who lives in Iowa. Her writing has been published in *Electric Literature, The Idaho Review, PANK, Carve, The Masters Review*, and others. Her flash "The De Facto Mother" won the 2022 Oxford Flash Fiction Prize, and her short fiction was a finalist for The Iowa Review Award in Fiction. She is an associate professor of English at Drake University.

Suzanne Dottino is a writer of fiction and plays. Her recent fiction, "Angel of Mercy," appeared in the *Bellevue Literary Review* and was nominated for a Pushcart Prize. Her plays have been Finalists in the Samuel French Short Play Competition and published in numerous journals.

Iris Jamahl Dunkle is an award-winning literary biographer, poet, and former Poet Laureate of Sonoma County, CA. Her latest books include the biography *Charmian Kittredge London: Trailblazer, Author, Adventurer* (University of Oklahoma Press, 2020) and poetry collection *West : Fire : Archive* (The Center for Literary Publishing, 2021). Find her work at www.irisjamahldunkle.com.

Olivia Dunn teaches writing at Skidmore College and her work has appeared in *The Pinch Journal, Seneca Review, The Nervous Breakdown, Jellyfish Review, River Teeth, Entropy*, and *McSweeney's*. She holds an MFA in Nonfiction Writing from the University of Iowa. She's working on a memoir about growing up in Albany, NY and writes a newsletter about pandemic parenthood at momblog.substack.com

Brad Efford is the founding editor of *wig-wag* and *The RS 500*. He lives and teaches in Berkeley, California.

William Fargason is the author of *Love Song to the Demon-Possessed Pigs of Gadara* (University of Iowa Press, 2020). His poetry has appeared in *Ploughshares*, *The Threepenny Review*, *JMWW*, *New England Review*, *Narrative*, and elsewhere. He earned a PhD in poetry from Florida State University. He lives in Towson, Maryland.

Robert Feldman—inspired by iconic members of hometown Paterson's literary tradition, most notably Allen Ginsberg and William Carlos Williams—found the Bisbee Poets Collective and helped facilitate the annual Bisbee Poetry. He continues to write / publish / present his work ("Hineni," "Sunflowers, Sutras, Wheatfields and other ArtPoems"), make fire paintings, and play tablas.

Jennifer Fliss (she/her) is a Seattle-based writer whose writing has appeared in numerous publications online and in print. She is the writer of *The Predatory Animal Ball* and *As If You Had a Say*, a short story collection forthcoming in 2023 from Northwestern University Press/Curbstone Books.

Jaime Fountaine was raised by "wolves." Her work has appeared in *PANK*, *littletell*, *Knee-Jerk*, and *Fanzine*. She lives in Philadelphia, where she co-hosts the Tire Fire reading series.

Emily Franklin's debut poetry collection, *Tell Me How You Got Here*, was published in 2021. Her work has appeared on NPR and in the *New York Times*, *Guernica*, *New Ohio Review*, *Cincinnati Review*, and *Alaska Quarterly Review* among other places. Her novel *The Lioness of Boston*, about the life Isabella Stewart Gardner, is forthcoming in 2023.

Temim Fruchter is a queer Jewish writer who lives in Brooklyn. She holds an MFA from the University of Maryland, and is the recipient of fellowships from the DC Commission on the Arts and Humanities and Vermont Studio Center, and a 2020 Rona Jaffe Foundation Writer's Award. More at www.temimfruchter.com.

Sherine Gilmour graduated with an MFA in poetry from New York University. She received a special mention in Pushcart 2022, and her poems have appeared in or are forthcoming from *Cleaver, The Indianapolis Review, Jet Fuel Review, Rogue Agent, Salamander,* and other publications.

Gwen Goodkin is the author of the short story collection, *A Place Remote,* recipient of a Silver IPPY Award. She has won the Folio Editor's Prize for Fiction as well as the John Steinbeck Award for Fiction. For more information, visit gwengoodkin.com

Eli Goldblatt's poems have appeared in small literary journals since 1972. His most recent poetry collection is *For Instance* (Chax P). His latest book in Writing Studies is *Literacy as Conversation* (U of Pittsburgh P), co-written with David Jolliffe. He is Professor Emeritus of English at Temple University in Philadelphia.

Christopher Gonzalez is the author of *I'm Not Hungry but I Could Eat* (SFWP 2021). He is a 2021 NYFA/NYSCA Artist Fellow in Fiction and serves as a fiction editor at *Barrelhouse* magazine. He lives mostly on Twitter: @livesinpage

Hannah Gordon is a writer, editor, and middle school teacher living in Chicago. Her work can be found at hannahngordon.com.

Anita Goveas is British-Asian, London-based, and fueled by strong coffee and paneer jalfrezi. She's on the editorial team at *Flashback Fiction,* an editor at Mythic Picnic's Twitter zine, and tweets erratically @coffeeandpaneer Her debut flash collection, *Families and other natural disasters,* is available from Reflex Press, and links to her stories are at https://coffeeandpaneer.wordpress.com

John Grey is an Australian poet, US resident, recently published in *Sheepshead Review, Stand, Poetry Salzburg Review,* and *Hollins Critic.* Latest books, *Leaves on Pages, Memory Outside The Head,* and *Guest Of Myself* are available through Amazon. Work upcoming in *Ellipsis, Blueline,* and *International Poetry Review.*

James Grinwis is the author of *The City from Nome* (National Poetry Review Press) and *Exhibit of Forking Paths* (Coffee House/National Poetry Series). He lives in Greenfield, MA.

Ben Gunsberg is a professor of English at Utah State University, where he directs the Graduate Specialization in Creative Writing. He's the author of the poetry collection *Welcome, Dangerous Life* and the chapbook *Rhapsodies with Portraits*. He moonlights as the multi-medium editor of *Sugar House Review.*

Katie Gutierrez has an MFA from Texas State University, and her writing has appeared in *The Washington Post, Longreads, Catapult, Electric Lit, LitHub*, and more. She is the author of *More Than You'll Ever Know* (Waterstones). Find her at: katiegutierrez.net.

Anna Gates Ha lives in Northern California. She earned her MFA from Saint Mary's College of California, and her work has appeared in *Fractured Lit, The Citron Review, Emerge Literary Journal*, among others

Joe Hall is the author of five books of poetry, including *Someone's Utopia* (2018) and *Fugue & Strike* (forthcoming). In addition to *jmww*, his poems, reviews, and scholarship have appeared in *Poetry Daily, Postcolonial Studies, Peach Mag, terrain.org, PEN America Blog, Poetry Northwest, Ethel Zine, Gulf Coast*, and *Best Buds! Collective.*

Amorak Huey's fourth book of poems is *Dad Jokes from Late in the Patriarchy* (Sundress Publications, 2021). Co-author with W. Todd Kaneko of the textbook, *Poetry: A Writer's Guide and Anthology* (Bloomsbury, 2018) and the chapbook, *Slash/Slash* (Diode, 2021), Huey teaches writing at Grand Valley State University in Michigan.

Kelsey Ipsen's work can be found in *PANK, Columbia Journal, Hobart, jmww, wigleaf.* and the *wigleaf Top 50 of 2020*. Originally from New Zealand she now lives and writes in France.

Dean P. Johnson has been writing journalism and teaching literature and writing for over 30 years. He has published essays in *The New York Times*, *Los Angeles Times*, *Washington Post*, *Christian Science Monitor*, and other newspapers, and creative nonfiction, short stories, and poetry in journals such as *Chronogram*, *Foundling Review*, *ArtWord Quarterly*, and more. He holds an MA in Writing from Rowan University.

Michele Finn Johnson's short fiction collection, *Development Times Vary*, was the winner of the 2021 Moon City Press Short Fiction Award and is forthcoming in 2022. Her work has appeared in *Colorado Review*, *Mid-American Review*, *DIAGRAM*, *2019 Best Small Fictions*, and else-where, and won an AWP Intro Journals Award. www.michelefinnjohnson.com @m_finn_johnson

Monty Jones is a writer in Austin. He has worked as a newspaper reporter and a university public affairs official and is the author of a volume of poetry, *Cracks in the Earth,* published in 2018 by Cat Shadow Press of Austin, as well as two books of non-fiction.

Jen Karetnick is the author/co-author of 21 books, including 11 volumes of poetry. Her creative writing and journalism appear widely. She is the co-founder and managing editor of SWWIM Every Day. Find her on Instagram at JenKaretnick, on Twitter at Kavetchnik, or at jkaretnick.com.

Katie Kemple lives in Southern California with her family. Her poems have appeared in recent issues of *Atlanta Review*, *Ligeia Magazine*, *Little Patuxent Review*, *The South Carolina Review*, and *The West Review*.

Leonard Kress has published poetry and fiction in *Iowa Review*, *American Poetry Review*, *Harvard Review*, etc. Recent collections: *Walk Like Bo Diddley*, *Living in the Candy Store*, and *Craniotomy Sestinas*. His new verse translation of the Polish Romantic epic, Pan Tadeusz, by Adam Mickiewicz, was published in 2018.

Rachel Kowalsky is a pediatric emergency physician and health humanities educator in New York City. She is a Pushcart Prize nominee and winner of the *New England Journal of Medicine*'s fiction contest. Her work can be found in *jmww*, *Atticus Review*, *The Intima*, *Orca*, *HerStry*, and elsewhere.

B. Tyler Lee is the author of *With Our Lungs in Our Hands* (Red Bird Chapbooks) and winner of the 2021 Best Spiritual Writing Anthology Award for poetry. Recent work has appeared in *Vassar Review*, *Blue Mesa Review*, *Whale Road Review*, and elsewhere. She can be found online at btylerlee.com.

Jane Lin is a poet and a software engineer for an environmental consulting company. Her first book, *Day of Clean Brightness*, was published by 3: A Taos Press. She is a Kundiman Fellow and has lived in Northern New Mexico for over two decades.

Davon Loeb is the author of the memoir *The In-Betweens* (West Virginia University Press, 2023). He earned an MFA in creative writing from Rutgers-Camden University. Davon is an assistant features editor at *The Rumpus*. His work is featured at *Joyland Magazine*, *The Rumpus*, *Catapult Magazine*, *Ploughshares Blog*, *JMWW*, and elsewhere. He can be reached on Twitter at @LoebDavon

Owen Lucas is a writer, teacher, and student of languages born in Britain and based in Connecticut. His poetry and translations have been published in the U.S., Britain, and Canada.

Cate McGowan, a Georgia native, is an essayist, poet, and fiction writer whose work appears in numerous literary outlets and anthologies. She is the author of the novel, *These Lowly Objects*, and the short story collection, *True Places Never Are*, which won the Moon City Press Short Fiction Award

DW McKinney writes and gardens in Nevada. Her work has appeared in *I'm Speaking Now* (Chicken Soup for the Soul, 2021), *Los Angeles Review*

of Books, Narratively, Hippocampus Magazine, McNeese Review, and *PANK*. She is a nonfiction editor for Shenandoah and editor-at-large for Raising Mothers. Say hello at dwmckinney.com.

Davis MacMillan lives with his wife and son in Jersey City, NJ.

Kelly McQuain's debut poetry collection, *Scrape the Velvet from Your Antlers*, was recently chosen by Texas Review Press for their Southern Breakthrough Series. His chapbook, *Velvet Rodeo*, won the Bloom prize. He is a Lambda Fellow and a Sewanee Scholar. Also a painter, he lives and works in Philadelphia. www.KellyMcQuain.word-press.com.

Sarah Jane Miller is a public librarian who loves living in Baltimore. Her work has appeared in *Void Magazine, Hidden City Quarterly, JMWW,* and issues of *Smile, Hon, You're in Baltimore*.

David Mohan is a poet and short story writer based in Dublin. His poetry has been published in *The Cincinnati Review, Spoon River Poetry Review, Lake Effect, Measure, Superstition Review, New World Writing,* and *PANK*. His poetry has been nominated for The Pushcart Prize and won the Christopher Hewitt Award. His first pamphlet, *Wildfire*, is forthcoming from Against the Grain Press.

Loren Moreno is a journalist and writer from Honolulu, Hawaii, living in New York City. He is a graduate of the MFA Creative Writing Program at The New School. He is also the author of the chapbook AARON & KEONI (Gertrude Press, 2013) and the founder of Atomic Theory Micro Press.

G.H. Mosson is the author of five books of poetry, including *Family Snapshot as a Poem in Time* (Finishing Line, 2019), and coauthor of *Simultaneous Revolutions* (PM Press, 2021). Mr. Mosson lives in Maryland, and enjoys raising his children, hiking, and literature. For more, seek www.ghmosson.com.

Jeremy Penna is the author of *Walls and Windows* (Forthcoming, 2024 Branton Press) and *Global Bearings: The Politics of International Order* (2022, Branton Press). He lives in Newark, Delaware, where he teaches English as a Second Language.

Jessica Pierce's debut collection, *Consider the Body, Winged*, was published by First Matter Press in 2021. Her poems have appeared in *Bellingham Review, Tar River Poetry, Painted Bride Quarterly,* and elsewhere. She has been a finalist for *CALYX*'s Lois Cranston Memorial Poetry Prize, *New Ohio Review*'s NORward Prize, and a two-time finalist for *Nimrod*'s Pablo Neruda Prize, among other awards.

Megan Pillow is project manager for Roxane Gay and co-editor of The Audacity. Her work has appeared or is forthcoming in, among other places, in *Electric Literature, SmokeLong Quarterly, Catapult, Brevity, The Believer, TriQuarterly, Guernica,* and *Gay Magazine* and has been featured in *Longreads*. She lives in Louisville, Kentucky with her two children.

Claire Polders is the author of four novels in Dutch and one novel for younger readers in English, *A Whale in Paris* (Simon & Schuster). Her short prose was published in *Prairie Schooner, Tin House, Electric Literature, TriQuarterly, Denver Quarterly,* and *Fiction International*. She blogs about traveling, books, and writing on www.clairepolders.com.

Kristen M. Ploetz lives in Massachusetts and is currently enrolled in Lesley University's low-res MFA program. Her short fiction was selected for inclusion in the 2020 Wigleaf Top 50, 2020 Best Small Fictions, and 2019 Best Microfiction anthologies and nominated for a Pushcart Prize. Find her at www.kristenploetz.com and Twitter (@KristenPloetz).

Suzanne S. Rancourt, a two-time Best of the Net Nominee, is of Abenaki/Huron descent. She has authored *Billboard in the Clouds* (Northwestern University Press), which received the Native Writers' Circle of the Americas First Book Award, as well as *murmurs at the gate* (Unsolicited Press, 2019) and *Old Stones, New Roads* (Main Street Rag Publishing,

2021). Her fourth book, *Songs of Archilochus* (Unsolicited Press) is forthcoming in 2023. For more, see her website: www.expressive-arts.com

Michael Ratcliffe's poems have appeared in various print and online journals. His chapbook, *Shards of Blue*, was published by Finishing Line Press in 2015. When he is not writing, he can be found managing census geographic programs or bicycling throughout Central Maryland. He can also be found at michaelratcliffespoetry.wordpress.com.

C. Samuel Rees is a queer Pennsylvania-born poet and MFA candidate with the New Writers Project in Austin, TX. His work excavates trauma, landscape, masculinity, queerness, contagion, lineage, complicity, and rurality. His work has appeared in *Territory, Action Books, Sonora Review, The Shore Poetry, Frontier Poetry*, and elsewhere.

Blake Z. Rong is a freelance writer, editor and journalist whose work has appeared in *Autoweek, Road & Track, Jalopnik, Automobile*, and *Petrolicious*, among other publications. He grew up in Massachusetts and holds an MFA from the Vermont College of Fine Arts. He lives in New York with a cat named Moose.

Cody Smith is the author of *Gulf: Poems* (Texas Review Press). He is a former Mississippi Review Prize and River Styx International Poetry Prize winner. His work has appeared in *Poetry, Prairie Schooner, Puerto del Sol*, and elsewhere.

Gary Sokolow has a long-ago MFA from Brooklyn College and currently works in finance. His poems have appeared in the *Connecticut River Review, Salamander, Posit, JMWW, 2 Bridges Review, Third Wednesday, Eye Flash Journal*, and other publications. He is currently working on his first book.

Chelsea Stickle is the author of the flash fiction chapbook *Breaking Points* (Black Lawrence Press, 2021). Her stories appear in *CHEAP POP, CRAFT, McSweeney's Internet Tendency, Best Microfiction 2021*, and others. She lives in Annapolis, MD with her black rabbit George. Read more at chelseastickle.com and on Twitter @Chelsea_Stickle.

Laurie Stone, a former longtime writer for the *Village Voice*, is the author of six books, most recently *Streaming Now, Postcards from the Thing that is Happening.*

Megan Stolz's writing explores loss, relationships, and spirituality. Her poetry has appeared in *Two Thirds North, Better Than Starbucks,* and others. She studied creative writing at the University of Baltimore and Hollins University. A Californian, she lives in the Washington, DC, suburbs with her family. Find more writing at https://www.meganstolzeditorial.com/creative-writing.

Hannah Storm's writing has placed second at the Bath Flash Fiction Award, been named in *Best Microfictions 2021,* the *BIFFY 50,* and nominated for *Best of the Net.* Her debut collection, *The Thin Line Between Everything and Nothing,* was published by Reflex Press and her memoir, *Aftershocks,* shortlisted in the 2021 Mslexia award.

Eve Strillacci, a graduate of the Hollins MFA program in Creative Writing, lives and writes in Queens, NY. Her work has appeared in *Sixth Finch, The RS 500, JMWW,* and elsewhere.

FM Stringer received an MFA from the University of Maryland. He lives in Pennsylvania.

Michael Sukach is the author of *Hypothetically Speaking, Something Impossible Happens,* and *Impression of a Life.* His poetry and reviews appear in several journals to include *Diagram, JMWW, Connotation Press, Spoon River Poetry Review, Construction Magazine, Yemassee,* and others. He is a retired Air Force officer living in Colorado.

Eshani Surya is a writer from Connecticut. Her writing has appeared in or is forthcoming in *[PANK], Catapult, Paper Darts, Joyland,* and *Literary*

Hub, among others. Eshani is an Assistant Flash Fiction Editor at *Split Lip Magazine.* She holds an MFA from the University of Arizona in Tucson. Find her @__eshani or at http://eshani-surya.com.

Brittany Terwilliger is Managing Editor at *Pithead Chapel* and her novel, *The Insatiables* (Chicago Review Press) was published in 2018. Her short fiction has been nominated for Best of the Net, Best Microfiction, the Pushcart Prize, and the Oxford Flash Fiction Prize. Find her on Twitter @Brttnyblm.

Cathy Ulrich is the founding editor of *Milk Candy Review,* a journal of flash fiction. Her work has been published in various journals and anthologies. She lives in Montana with her daughter and hardly any small animals.

Anthony Varallo is the author of a novel, *The Lines* (University of Iowa Press), as well as four short story collections. His stories have appeared in *The New Yorker* "Daily Shouts," *One Story, The Sun, STORY, Gulf Coast, X-R-A-Y,* and elsewhere. Find him online at @TheLines1979.

Jemimah Wei is a 2022-4 Stegner Fellow, a 2020 De Alba Fellow, and a Francine Ringold Award for New Writers Honouree. Her fiction has been nominated for the Pushcart Prize, recognized by the Best of the Net Anthologies, and has appeared in *Narrative, Nimrod,* and *CRAFT Literary,* among others.

Monica Wendel is the author of *No Apocalypse* (Georgetown Review Press, 2013) and *English Kills* (Autumn House Press, 2019). Her poetry has appeared in the *Bellevue Literary Review, Ploughshares,* and other journals. She is an associate professor of composition and creative writing at St. Thomas Aquinas College.

Amy Kiger-Williams holds an MFA in Fiction from Rutgers-Newark. Her work has appeared in *Yale Review, South Carolina Review, Chicago Quarterly Review,* and elsewhere. She is at work on a novel.

Devon Wootten's work has appeared in *Best American Experimental Writing, Fence,* and *LIT,* among other journals. He has an MFA from the University of Montana and a PhD from the University of Iowa and curates bestamericanyou.com and wikipoesis.com. He lives with his wife and daughter in Prague.

Dana Yost was an award-winning daily newspaper journalist for 29 years. Since 2008, he has published eight books, most recently the novel *Before I Get Old.* He is a three-time nominee for the Pushcart Prize in poetry. He lives in Sioux Falls, SD.

Xueyi Zhou was born and raised in Foshan, a city of manufacturing in Guangdong, China. She is currently pursuing her MFA at UNLV. Her fiction has appeared or is forthcoming in *Guernica, Waxwing, Passages North, Chestnut Review, Tahoma Lit Review, AAWW The Margins,* and more.

Laura A. Zink earned her MFA from St. Mary's College of California and her MA in English from the University of Minnesota Duluth. Her fiction has appeared in *Broad River Review, Full of Crow, sPARKLE & bLINK, Naked Bulb 2016 Summer Anthology, Literally Stories,* and *FICTION on the WEB.*